Angel Child

by Apara Mahal Sylvester

Published by CreateSpace

Cover design by Apara Mahal Sylvester

Edited by Christi Kelly and Kate Price

ISBN-13:
978-1508968726

ISBN-10:
1508968721

Table of Contents

Foreword

You have opened a book devoid of pretense and filled with truthful presence. "AngelChild" is about one person's journey to the center of her being through the turbulence of manic episodes. For the thoughtful reader, it could just as well be about a universal path to a place of stillness hidden within each of us.

Especially in this generation of hyper-stimulation, finding peace is a matter of discipline and intention. For those with wide mood swings, the search for center is initially about stability and functionality. Like most challenges in life, hidden in adversity is the blessing of awakening consciousness.

Through the author's dark moments rings humor. Through her sense of emptiness comes the fullness of self-acceptance. The paradox of opposites resolves in the center; the balancing point. Here the pendulum stops swinging for all of us.

"AngelChild" is about finding the golden threads in the tapestry of life experience. It is about transcending confusion and finding clarity. Finally, it is about overcoming fear through courage and love.

Rosanne A. Bostonian, Ph.D. April, 2015

Chapter 1

Awakening

February 9th 2010

That night there was a bad blizzard outside and I drove off into the dense and blinding snow many miles from home. I was on the road to nowhere, thinking I was supposed to die.

I want to stress I was NOT suicidal, that much I knew. There is a BIG difference between preparing for and planning to execute the termination of your own life vs. thinking or feeling that you are supposed to die.

My hope was gone that night, and during my drive to nowhere I was listening to music and smoking what I thought was my last cigarette. I kept thinking about my (now) husband whom I had only just met and I was so incredibly sad that I would never see him again or have a chance with him.

There are two versions of what happened next, one I remember and one that was told to me. I was told I hit some sort of truck. All of a sudden, my car spun around in slow motion and hit a guardrail. My airbag deployed upon impact. The next thing I remember was stillness and quiet. My eyes were closed and I didn't know if I was dead.

Next I heard a familiar voice, the voice of my friend Milo. He uttered one single word:

"Awake"

I opened my eyes and realized that I was not dead.

I awoke that night. This is the night I was reborn. This night made me who I am today.

Chapter 2

Ascent into Mania

I now know that the night of my car accident I was in a state of severe mania and an altered mental status. I don't know or remember what triggered this most severe event I had ever experienced. The thing with mania is that you're full in it, but because your mind is affected, you don't know you're in it so time, place and events can't be calculated.

Despite being in a severe state of mania, I knew exactly what was going on but had no control over my thoughts or actions. As I read now what I have written, it sounds so bizarre, but with mania you truly are on the outside looking in. Somehow you are aware of your thoughts, speech and actions but if something is amiss, you are totally out of control to change it and mania is all amiss.

After the accident, which totaled my beloved Jaguar but thankfully not me, I got out of the car and two vehicles stopped to see if I was ok. A man offered to drive me home and I accepted his ride. A person in their right state of mind would never have accepted a ride from a stranger, but my mind was not my own that night. Luckily, this man was extremely kind. He drove me well out of his way to get me home and safe.

When I abandoned my car I left my handbag and cell phone inside. I later learned the police had conducted a search for me for four hours thinking I was injured or dead and had walked off into the woods. I also know the police called whatever numbers they could on my phone's recent call list so my close friends, and my parents, did not know what happened to me for a period of time. I can't imagine what anguish my loved ones felt. I cannot feel guilty though because none of it was my fault.

I slept on my sofa that night and I recall having warm, pleasant dreams. When I woke up I was confused as to what happened. I was also in pain, which ultimately led me to seek medical attention at a local hospital. From there I was sent to a mental facility for three weeks of treatment.

No one told me what I was there for, so one day I asked the staff psychiatrist. He responded:

Manic bipolar.

I mentally shrugged and said "Oh, ok." I accepted what I was told. I don't know why this was my reaction but, for me, acceptance was the first step to moving forward and healing.

Some call my condition manic bipolar, but since I do not go downward into depression I simply call it mania. I have a mild form, per my psychiatrist, but it's enough to cause damage if left untreated.

I don't know when my mania set in. I think it developed in my 20s, but I was formally diagnosed in 2010 and put on Lithium, which I take without fail. Luckily, I only had one severe manic episode that I wish I could forget, but nevertheless I wrote about it because it changed my life.

If you're not aware of or are not looking for the symptoms, then you can't pinpoint their onset. I can't look back in time and say "On January 13th 2000 I said something really odd and nonsensical to my mother and this was when my mania started." It just doesn't work that way. Chemical imbalances are not like the common cold. My common colds are like an exact science and the outcome can easily be predicted. One minute I will feel fine and the next minute I will feel feverish, and that is the onset that will tire out my body and retire me to the sofa or bed for one or two days' rest.

Lithium became my friend and my protective "shield" over the mania. It keeps my head even and prevents the "alien" inside my brain from coming out. I stole the word alien from a dear friend, as it really is the most appropriate word to describe something that takes over your brain and renders it out of your control such as untreated or exacerbated mania does.

I suppose saying that having manic bipolar as opposed to manic depressive bipolar is a blessing sounds crazy (no pun intended), but it really is. The moderate manic highs increased my productivity, which helped me in stressful jobs, especially one time when preparing to move to London on a short work assignment. It allowed me to work late hours into the evening and return bright and early the next morning.

Though there is no cure for mania or any other chemical imbalances (as I prefer to call them), I speak of the events of my past as if they didn't really happen to me and I am in fact guessing. My parents, in hindsight, can point out instances of manic episodes based on the symptoms we all now know. For me, the mania was unconscious behavior, so I'm not able to pinpoint situations in life where it emerged. It was a part of who I was. It will always be a part of me but thanks to the help I received, as well as a daily dose of Lithium, I am ok now.

Chapter 3

My Race Is My Humanity

My father is Northern Indian, born and raised in India. My mother is half Polish and half Slovak, born and raised in the USA. I was born in New Delhi, India, in 1974. My father and mother met when both worked for Revlon cosmetics and married in 1971. At the time I was born, my parents were living in India as my father had wanted to start a business there. As both were United States citizens, I was considered an American citizen born abroad. I came back to the USA three months after birth.

Many years later, when I was applying to graduate school, the school I was accepted into would not recognize the United States Department of State Certificate of Birth Abroad. I had to go to the local Immigration and Naturalization office with all of my documents to obtain an official Certificate of Citizenship. In fact, I actually became a U.S. citizen twice; once on the day of my birth and the other on July 24th 1996 when I was handed my Certificate of Citizenship by and Immigration clerk who said "Congratulations on becoming a U.S. citizen." Twenty-two years later, that was a really nice thing to hear, and I could appreciate how newly naturalized immigrant citizens must feel.

My father is a practicing Sikh, a monotheistic religion. My mother is a non-practicing Catholic, also a monotheistic religion. Growing up I was taught Sikhism at home and Catholicism at school. I was taught by my parents that I could be both religions and it was ok to practice both. To a small child this caused nothing but mass confusion in my little child mind. Though both Sikhs and Catholics believe in one God, at bedtime I used to say both Catholic and Sikh prayers, thinking that if I skipped a prayer I would be unfaithful to God – the same God, mind you.

Sikhs don't cut their hair because they believe hair is a gift from God, so I was not allowed to have cut hair as a child. I wanted to have short hair with bangs like my classmates, and because I wasn't allowed to it made me feel different. When it was time for all the children in my class to make their first holy communion, I begged my parents to let me participate so I too could wear a white lace frilly dress, but my pleas fell onto deaf ears. I would sit in church and read books while the other children practiced for their ceremony. I was baptized, though, as a baby. I don't know how my mother pulled that one off. I later learned I was baptized with my father's consent.

Growing up I would say I had the typical identity crisis of a child with mixed race parents: Who am I and where do I belong? To this day, I still don't know. Having lived in three countries outside of the USA (four if you want to count my three months in India as an infant) I like to consider myself a world citizen. I've been told I look Spanish, Italian, Egyptian and Greek. Rarely Indian and never Polish or Slovak.

I do tell people my ethnic background, but most people either forget what I told them or only choose to remember one part of me, which is usually Indian. My response to those who call me Indian is I have a mother too, and she is Polish and Slovak and together with my Indian father. That's what I am.

Years ago when I was looking for government jobs I was interviewed by the FBI. I did not get to go further in their process as I did not possess their critical language skills needed at that time. Too bad for the feds, because with my looks I could blend in with half the world's population, and I think I would have made a darn good undercover agent. Alas, it was not meant to be and it was not my true calling.

On forms where you see race and ethnicity fields, there used to be no box to categorize me. Somehow my employer payroll has me down as Asian, which is incorrect. I'm guessing they thought that based on my name.

I'm very impressed though with the new Race and Ethnicity form as proposed by the U.S. Census

Bureau, where at least you can check off multiple boxes that apply.

When I receive the new census form I think I will check the last box only: "Some other race or origin." I may say my race is humanity. That sounds pretty good.

Regardless, putting myself in a box never was my style. I prefer breaking out of boxes and soaring like the free bird that I am.

Chapter 4

I Want To Be Like Mrs. Farmer

Growing up I was the only child among many adults, therefore it was no surprise that I was quite mature beyond my tender years. Up to the age of 10, I lived with my parents in the home of my grandparents. One of my dearest childhood friends was a woman who lived a few houses down from my grandparents, named Mrs. Farmer.

Mrs. Farmer was slightly younger than my grandparents and she was a columnist for the local newspaper. She wrote a short weekly column titled "Glowing With Age" which focused on senior citizens. Her columns were light and humorous. I would go visit her house almost daily, and she would always warmly welcome me inside.

One of my fondest memories of Mrs. Farmer was taking her dog Harry for a walk inside a beautiful old cemetery in our town. The cemetery was built on a rolling hillside. It was peaceful and quiet. I enjoyed the serene strolls Mrs. Farmer and I took, and I enjoyed peering at all of the intricately carved old tombstones.

Saturday mornings, Mrs. Farmer and I would sometimes drive around and descend upon local yard sales. Another person's junk is someone else's treasure, and hunting for yard sale treasures was a passion we mutually enjoyed.

I believe Mrs. Farmer wrote this recommendation letter for my first job at a local hospital. This letter best exemplifies my childhood up to age 17:

To Whom It May Concern:

There are among us, those persons who even at a young age cause us to say, "You'll be something someday!" This had been said to Apara not just by me but also others, as I have learned.

Even at age eight when Apara extended a friendly though reserved greeting upon my move into the neighborhood where she lived with her parents, her grandparents, and close Aunt – even then, an impression was that this self-assured, much-loved-by-family child would go far.

A first surprise was that Apara could hold a give and take conversation with any adult regardless of age. Yet, she was popular with those of her own age.

Apara liked to read. Her own home library, the books lining her room and the family den, ranged from children's classics to fun books and light novels, encyclopedias, and the works of noted authors that may have been a challenge for her to read and comprehend.

The books, her parents were quick to point out, were mostly of her own choosing.

Like her parents, Apara took an active interest in her town and became a member of organizations like the W.A.T.E.R. group whose efforts resulted in the naming of the Perth Amboy ferry slip as a historical landmark. (She was the youngest member of the group.)

Apare is also a member of the Heritage Ball series of annual events that promotes understanding among the many ethnic groups throughout New Jersey. In time, she has become a committee leader.

Apara has maintained a high scholastic average and is conscientious about studying. This is not to imply that she has a nerd-like seriousness. On the contrary! She has a lively personality! And she can charm even the most intractable opponent!

Now, as a young person on the threshold of adulthood, Apara wants to join the ranks of those who must work. She has a consummate willingness to learn and to do a good job.

And it pleases me to be recommending Apara for her employment with you.

In reference to the historic Perth Amboy ferry slip, below is a painting of that very ferry slip I acquired, which was painted by a local Perth Amboy Artist by the name of Tom Ward. I always admired Tom's artwork and wanted one of his pieces for years, and now this painting of the ferry slip proudly hangs on my living room wall.

When I was in my late teens, Mrs. Farmer retired and moved to Florida. We wrote letters for a while but then lost touch. I think of her fondly to this day, and it would not be befitting if I did not dedicate a chapter of my book to her. Mrs. Farmer was a columnist and a novelist. She was a lovely, kind-hearted woman who accepted a little girl decades younger than her as her friend and invited her into her world.

Mrs. Farmer believed I would be something someday. I am something, Mrs. Farmer. I am a writer, just like you.

Chapter 5

Child of the Universe

"You are a child of the Universe"

- Desiderata

Jan Weber was my 4th grade teacher, and she took a special liking to me. Among the many gifts she gave me was the Desiderata in book form, which I still cherish to this day.

Mrs. Weber wasn't necessarily my favorite teacher but she became an important part of my life. She was a tough teacher who took a special, though not in any way preferential, interest in me and always encouraged me to read and write.

I remember one class project where she had each of us write a story in a book of blank pages she gave us so we would have authored a book of our own. I always thought that was very special. Every teacher should do such a project with their students; Allow them to freely create their own book to be proud of and say they had written all by themselves. I wish I still had a copy of my book from class.

Mrs. Weber was only at my grammar school for about a year. After she left, we wrote letters to each other and became friends. I would meet up with her from time to time and she always gave me small gifts, some of which I still have to this day. My favorite present is a little toy squeaky pig, which she named "Pretty Petunia." In class she taught us about prisms and gave me one, which I used to place on my windowsill and admire the rainbow beam that shone through.

She used to send me a lot of personalized bookmarks as well. The front side of one reads: "Anything is possible if only you believe." On the back Mrs. Weber inscribed: "To know. To learn. To care." The backside of another says: "To Apara, a child of The Universe and more."

Whenever I write a book chapter, I always listen to a song that reminds me of a person, place or event. Mrs. Weber passed away in 1997. For her chapter, I played her favorite song: "I Have A Dream" by Abba. I felt her looking down at me and smiling.

After her death her daughter Marilyn sent me a note with just one sentence on it:

"Apara, she loved you."

I wish Mrs. Weber were here today so she could read my stories and see my published book come to fruition, but I know she is always with me in spirit.

Mrs. Weber and I ca. 1996

Chapter 6

A Writer in the Making

It's hard for me to recall exactly when I developed an interest and passion for writing. I recall as a child always writing letters to relatives overseas and I even had penpals overseas whom I wrote to. I was also an avid reader and my absolute favorite books were the Ramona Quimby series by Beverly Cleary. I also enjoyed all Laura Ingalls Wilder Little House on the Prairie books.

Once when I was about 10 or 12 my parents and I took a trip to California. On a tour bus we met a lovely older woman from Australia. As I was the same age as her granddaughter, Tracy. She gave me Tracy's address and we began a long correspondence. At this time there was no internet.

Now, Tracy and I are connected on social media some 30 years later. It's amazing the connections you retain in life.

My parents saved much of my childhood and teenage writing samples which they later turned over to me and which is how I found "Blood Roses." Initially I wasn't certain when I wrote this story so I had to ask my fifth grade teacher, Mrs. Slicner, if this was her handwriting. That is correct; I am still in touch with my fifth grade teacher, as are many of my former grammar school classmates, all thanks to social media.

Mrs. Slicner was the beautiful, kind funny teacher whom we all loved. To this day she remembers each and every little detail from when we were students in her class.

I remember she used to always come to class fashionably dressed with matching accessories and perfectly styled long brown hair. I'm notorious for having a poor memory but, aside from remembering Mrs. Slicner's kindness, I remember her once bringing in a baby shark preserved in formaldehyde in a jar which utterly fascinated me. Every child should be blessed with a teacher such as Mrs. Slicner.

Mrs. Slicner told me that, based on the way this paper was graded, that I must have written it in high school so I'm estimating that this was freshman year.

Blood Roses

It was the most cheerless house
to be seen in the small town. It's
medium frame was set back into the
thickest of the woods. The house
itself was made of wood and throughout
the years it had dilapidated greatly
and looked almost uninhabitable. The
lawn was overgrown with crabgrass and
weeds. The only bright spot on the
property was a small garden full of
bright pink rosebushes which grew on
the side of the house. Aside from
that, the property resembled a tiny
jungle. Passersby who see the house
first stare at it in pity, then walk
by with pensive looks on their faces.
They all think of the house's
inhabitants, the Chamberlains.

Going back twenty years of so,
Everett and Martha Chamberlain were
both well-known in the town. They ran
the local drugstore, and Everett was
best known for his remedies for every
ailment. The Chamberlain house then
was well-kept, cheery, and very

inviting. The Chamberlains had been a
lonely couple though, since they were
both in their forties and had no
children. But it was a joy to them
when Martha finally became pregnant
and had a baby boy, Michael. He meant
everything to them. Michael was
always seen around the drug store, but
he especially loved Martha's rose
garden at the house. He was
fascinated by their color and shapes.
He could stare in awe at them for
hours. Michael also loved animals.
He would play with all the local
people's pets, and he cared for them
greatly. He was the best little boy
anyone could want.

But one night, Martha and Everett
came screaming into town. It seemed
Michael had somehow gotten out of the
house and run off someplace. A search
party was formed, people searched all
night, but Michael was never seen
again. A few days later, his little
sock was found floating in a brook,
but Michael was never seen again. It
was after this that the Chamberlains
changed drastically. Everett and

Martha closed down their shop, became
isolated from the down, and lived in
seclusion, mourning their son.
Everything they took pride in went
away, especially in their house. The
only thing that thrived was the
rosegarden. IT served as a living
memorial of Michael. And so this has
remained for twenty years.

Recently, animals around the town
started to disappear one by one.
First it was Polly Merrill's dearly
loved poodle. Then, it was Jack
Schaffer's cat. No one knew what was
happening. Posters were going up all
around town, ads kept appearing in the
lost and found, but to no avail.
People all over town inquired about
the animals. "Hey Jack, any lck with
finding Muffin? Any news at all?"
Concerned people would ask. "No, thank
you for asking. If I find out
anything, I'll let you know." Jack
regretfully replied. Polly Merrill's
luck was no better. "Gee, Polly, I'm
really sorry about Frenchy. She'll
turn up, don't worry." Polly couldn't

even thank anyone. She would always burst into tears whenever she heard the name of her beloved Frenchy.

One day a citizen Kane, was walking past Chamberlain house. He saw something shimmering in the weeds. When he investigated, he found a diamond dog collar, spattered with blood. As he was investigating the collar, Mr. Kane heard sounds corning from the house. He listened carefully, and, if he was not mistaken, the sounds were that of cutting stone and of someone groaning in agony. Too terrified to investigate, Mr. Kane took the collar and dashed off as quickly as he could. But, he was very curious as well. Gaining courage, he returned to the Chamberlain house the next night and again heard the same disturbing sounds. Knowing that animals had been disappearing around town, Mr. Kane took the collar to the sheriff's office. Sheriff Murphy was puzzled by this discovery since the collar belonged to Polly Merrill's Frenchy and that the Chamberlains lived far from her. He was even more puzzled and suspicious when Mr. Kane spoke about the unusual noises, so he decided to investigate.

The sheriff, along with deputy, Brown, approached the Chamberlain house one evening around seven. Sheriff knocked on the door, and Martha Chamberlain Answered. She was dressed in her usual black garb, and had a sullen look on her face. Yes, gentlemen, may I help you?" She said with a coldness in her voice•.The sheriff spoke. "Good evening ma'am. Sorry to bother you at this hour. Deputy Brown and I would like to talk with you and your husband for a moment concerning a bloodied dog collar of a missing dog found on your property." Martha's voice lost a bit of its coldness. "Well, gentlemen, my husband is occupied at the moment and I cannot disturb him. I have no idea how a bloodied collar got on our property. We never see animals around here. I'm terribly sorry gentlemen."

Martha seemed a bit anxious as she spoke and her hands were trembling. Well then, Mrs. Chamberlain, perhaps you could tell us what was going on last night at your place. A citizen passing through seemed to have heard sounds of breaking stone and person yelling in pain. Can you explain this?" sheriff Murphy would not let up. As if on cue, all of a sudden, the sound of moaning and stone being chipped could be heard from the basement. It lasted for a few minutes, stopped briefly, then started up again. It sounded as if a human was in extreme pain and agony. "Good God, woman! What in the hell is that sound!" Deputy Brown and Sherriff Murphy demanded. "Nothing, nothing. Everett must have hurt his finger chipping stone. He makes stone sculptures, you know, and quite often he injures himself." Martha now was losing control of herself, voice trembling, face turning pale, and her hands were shaking faster than ever. Pushing Martha aside, Sheriff Murphy and Deputy Brown rushed to the basement door, flung it open, and bounded down the stairs. It was there in the Chamberlain basement that Sheriff Murphy and Deputy Brown saw the most horrible sight they were ever to witness.

The basement reeked of rotting flesh, so much so that Deputy Brown vomited from the stench. In the far corner stood a petrified Everett Chamberlain near a stone chopping block, ax in hand, with a terrified look on his face. On the block lay half the blood-soaked and mutilated remains of an animal, possibly a cat. Il around the basement floor bits of white fur, animal nails, and bones were scattered about in orderly war. There were also dead rosebuds soaked in blood placed upon a black ribbon near another corner of the basement. It was there a man was chained by his hands and legs. The man wore tattered brown pants and a tattered brown shirt. He was barefoot and his hair was long and matted. His overall appearance was unkempt. The man was screaming in distress at the torture going on to all that he loved around him. This man was Michael Chamberlain.

The End

Pretty graphic, yet also suspenseful — poor ol' Mike!

Interesting character depiction

A $\frac{48}{50}$

When I read this story all I could do was laugh at my imagination! I didn't watch crime shows on television when I was younger nor did I read true crime novels so I don't know how I came up with the plot. Perhaps, subconsciously, I wanted to one day be a detective. For a great many years of my youth I had my heart set on being a criminal justice lawyer.

I have no recollection of the house described in the story. It probably was one of the neighborhood homes. It was not the home I grew up in.

The character names especially made me smile and reminisce as to how I chose them. "Frenchy" was certainly from the character in Grease, one of my favorite movies.

Chamberlain had to have come from the actor Richard Chamberlain whose 1983 TV miniseries "The Thorn Birds" I was obsessed with. Imagine this scenario: Catholic school girl's favorite TV miniseries ever is about a love affair between a woman and a priest. Even though I'll probably be damned to hell for this one I am proud to say I have the miniseries' 25th anniversary edition DVD in my home and "The Thorn Birds" miniseries is one of the best miniseries I have ever seen to date.

Martha was a great aunt of mine and Michael was the name of my grandfather. Michael, in my story, is like myself and my great love of animals, especially cats.

I had the biggest laugh of all when I showed "Blood Roses" to my husband Johnny. The first sentence to come out of his mouth was:

"Are you going to kill me or something? A student don't write s**t like this!"

He also said he knew from the beginning that Michael was still alive.

What can I say…I was always very mature for my age, and maybe even a good writer from the get-go. My teacher gave me an "A" on my paper so she didn't consider me to be a sadistic teenager.

No, Johnny. I'm not going to kill you. I love you!

Chapter 7

Grandpa's Hands

"No thinking – that comes later. You must write your first draft with your heart. You rewrite with your head. The first key to writing is….to write, not think!"

- "Finding Forrester" (2000)

As we grow into adulthood, we shed many things from our past, and many things become distant memories. Our childhood is one of those memories. As time moves on, our youth becomes lost as the years pass by us like the hands of a clock. But the memories of people who touched our lives continue to linger on; time stands suspended. They live within us and become part of our soul and who we are. This is something time cannot take away.

Looking back into my own childhood, many events seem like a dream. As an adult, I can hardly believe I ever was young. However, when I think of my grandfather, my life is permanently locked into time. The memories of him all rush back to me, and once again I have my childhood restored for a brief moment, and he is present once again in my life.

I called him Grandpa.

For as far back as my mind can take me, he always looked the same. Mainly bald (as many grandfathers are) but still sporting a crew cut, which revealed the liver spots on his head. Soft brown eyes that always seemed to sparkle. Stocky build, and a slow and graceful walk, even with the cane he sometimes needed. I could say he was a strong man as a youth, yet as an elderly man he was not frail. However, I never thought of him in his youth; I thought of him as I knew him. I thought of him as Grandpa.

His best quality was his disposition. He wasn't a man to walk around smiling; he mainly looked stern. Yet, when his smile came out, it was short, brief, but noticed. He had a wonderful smile. When he laughed, his laugh could fill a whole room. But, like his smile, it was brief but noticed; a short chuckle, but one to be acknowledged.

He laughed the most when he was with his friends and family from "the old country." During those times, Grandpa laughed a lot. Sitting around the table, chatting in Polish, sharing memories and the past. It was wonderful to see him so alive and joyful.

Most other times though, Grandpa was cranky, even a bit crotchety, one could say. He had a right to be. He lived a long and hard life, and he was entitled to be any which way he wanted. As an adult, I can recognize these prominent characteristics. As a child, this was the way he was; the way I knew him; the way I loved him.

His favorite expression was "Ach, God Dammit!" which he said when he was annoyed, which was quite often. But he was always kind to me. He reprimanded me as a child when I did something wrong, but he never made me cry, and tears are something a child never forgets. I never had reason to cry with Grandpa.

When I was very young, he used to go fishing a lot. He would come home and immediately go to the basement with his treasures of the day. I, being as curious as a cat, would go down to the basement as well to see exactly what those hidden treasures were. One of my greatest pleasures as a child was to watch Grandpa "gut" the fish he caught. I always hated fish, especially the smell. But I would bear the smell just to watch Grandpa skillfully prepare his catch to be cooked for the night's meal. I never ate the fish he caught, but I watched almost every one of them being dissected.

Grandpa was a gardener as well, and every summer his garden would be brimming with a virtual forest of tomato plants, peppers, kohlrabe, and other vegetables. He was faithful to his charges, and most times during the day he could be found walking about tending his garden. I loved to follow him into his maze of greens, carefully stepping about on the planks he carefully placed as walkways leading to the vegetable plots. However, I could never stay in this maze for very long. Grandpa had business to do, and my curiosity and careless feet were a constant threat to his prized greens. Many a time I got a stern look and was chased back out into the yard. I never dared enter the garden when Grandpa wasn't there either; you never did know when he was watching from inside, and he never failed to catch me.

However, the garden wasn't Grandpa's only treasure trove. His garage and basement workshop were equally fascinating. Both were stocked full of everything: tools, nuts, bolts, boxes and many other knick-knacks. To the adult world, all this was just many years of collected things that should have been thrown out. But if you lived through the war, you learned not to throw anything out. In my young view, there were sure to be some hidden treasures buried somewhere within the rubble. As I said earlier, Grandpa had earned the right to do as he pleased, and his actions weren't questioned.

To me, the garage, even more than the basement, was a secret wonderland. If I had gone into it even a hundred times, each time everything would look just as if I had seen it for the first time. For Grandpa, my presence in the garage and basement didn't seem as threatening as the garden, so I was ok to marvel in there. But, just as the garden, I never dared go when Grandpa wasn't around. He was always sure to catch me with his watchful eyes.

In the physical world, there comes a time when God chooses to bring each one of us home to him. Grandpa's time came as well at the beginning of the New Year 1992.

Death is something humans will never be able to totally accept as just the way life has to be. People always question why and wish for even a few more moments with their loved one before they are gone from the physical world forever.

I didn't question Grandpa's death. In another sense, I felt luckier than most. I had the chance to say goodbye.

He was hospitalized, and I visited him on the night of his passing. There were tubes in his mouth, and he could not verbally communicate. But he was agitated; he didn't want me to see him that way. Grandpa never wanted me to feel pain.

Before I left his room, I got to tell him I loved him. I might not have realized it at that moment, but this was to be the last time I would see Grandpa. Later that night, my family got the call that he was gone. I was sad, but I felt privileged as well. For one last time, I had the chance to tell him I loved him.

The day of his funeral, there were many flowers around his casket. In his hands, he was holding mine. It was an arrangement of small pink and red roses in the shape of a heart. He took my heart with him when he was lowered into the ground. He had a part of me which not even death could take away. He had my heart.

That night as I slept, I dreamed of Grandpa. He was sitting on the porch in his favorite spot as he normally did on a warm day. Behind him, the sun shone brightly down around his body. He had a torn undershirt on and a pair of shorts, and he was holding his cane. And he was smiling. I knew he was at peace, and when I woke up, I was also at peace.

There is still one more memory of Grandpa time cannot take away. One day, several years before when he was hospitalized on another occasion, my mother came home from visiting him. She told me his doctor had brought a group of student doctors over to look at his hands, and that they were fascinated by them.

I asked my mother, "What did they want to look at his hands for?"

She seemed surprised and replied "Because they're deformed from arthritis. The doctors were amazed to see hands like that. Didn't you know this?"

What should I have known? I only knew Grandpa.

Grandpa caring for his vegetables as if they were his own children. Grandpa painstakingly kneading bread for our holiday meal. Grandpa faithfully writing letters to his relatives. Grandpa, only Grandpa.

"No," I replied.

I only knew they were Grandpa's hands.

Grandpa and I in 1975

Chapter 8

I Found the Needle in the Haystack

"Sally always said, life is a series of arrivals and departures"

-"View from the Top" (2003)

This "story" was actually my goodbye letter to my colleagues at one of my last corporate jobs at an international relocation company in 2007.

Everyone knows the saying "You can't find a needle in a haystack." I researched the origin of this saying and found that the needle actually refers to a short piece of hay which, among all the long stems of hay, is almost impossible to find. The exact definition of the expression is "A near impossible search for something." To use the word "can't," therefore, is actually not correct. My career in International Human Resources/Relocations actually began because I did find the needle in the haystack.

My "International Career" started exactly 10 years ago in August 1997. I had just completed a Masters degree in Health Policy and Management and I was preparing to move to Beijing, PRC to become an English teacher at a university there. I had five years of experience working in a hospital admitting office part time but no teaching experience whatsoever. Back then I never even thought of moving out of the state of New Jersey let alone halfway across the world. I was purely following a dream.

I always had a fascination with China and, when I visited Beijing for the first time in May 1997, I fell in love with it and wanted to work there. That became my goal. A professor of mine told me if I wanted to work in China, the best thing to do would be an English teacher. This professor was just giving me some advice. Little did I know how far her advice would carry me.

I went on the internet every night researching schools in Beijing and applying for teaching jobs. It was a stab in the dark and most people thought it would never happen. I knew it would happen but there was one time when I almost gave up hope.

One day in July, 1997, I had taken some advice from a Chinese businessman on how to get a job in China and he told me that without knowing Chinese it would be difficult, if not impossible. That night I was watching a movie alone in my bedroom which I couldn't concentrate on because the thoughts going through my mind were, "What if he is right? What if I can't make my dream happen?" That very same night, the one and only time I doubted that my dream could become a reality, I received a call from a university in Beijing offering me a teaching position for the fall 1997 semester.

The rest is history.

I made the near impossible possible. I spent two years in Beijing and I loved being a teacher. Those two years are still the best two years of my life.

After China I spent two years in Germany before moving back to the US in 2001. The US job market was tough and with all of my international experience it was not easy to find a job. One day, a family friend who worked at Siemens sent me a job description for an International Human Resources Consultant where two of the requirements were "Preferably lived overseas. Preferably speaks German." I never heard of International Human resources but the minute I saw that job description I said, "That job is mine."

The rest is history.

I've worked in International HR/Relocations 6 years. It has been interesting and challenging and I've met many wonderful people along the way. However, in all my six years of working in International HR/Relocations, I never really felt the pure satisfaction which teaching had brought me when I was in China. I love teaching and I decided that this is what I really want to do. Teaching/Training on a full time basis became my goal. It was not easy to achieve without any sold formal training background but I did not give up on my dream and goal. Once again I managed to make the impossible possible which now, 10 years later, brings an end to my "International Career" and begins my new career in Human Resources Training and Development.

I wish I could say "the rest is history" but my new history has not started yet. You'll need to check back with me in a few years!

As today is my last day you could say that this is my goodbye email to all of you since I may not be able to see all of you personally before I leave. Goodbye seems so final and I don't like saying goodbye. The world is small and you never know when you will meet again. It is now that I'd like to share one last story with you about saying goodbye.

Ray is a Canadian who I met in Beijing in 1997. Helen is an American who moved to Beijing and became Ray's girlfriend and who I met in 1998. I said goodbye to Ray and Helen when I left China in 1999. The next time I saw Ray was in the summer 2001 at a coffee shop in Manhattan when he was visiting Helen who had moved back to Manhattan. I attended Ray and Helen's engagement party in Manhattan in December 2003. I was at their wedding on Martha's Vineyard in June 2004. The last time I saw Ray and Helen was in December 2005 when I visited their home in New Jersey. Ray and Helen are now back working in China and we chat occasionally on Yahoo messenger. I don't know when I'll see them again but, as the world is small, I'll meet up with them somewhere eventually.

In conclusion, I would only like to tell you don't give up on any of your dreams and goals no matter what anyone may tell you because you can make the impossible possible. Always keep one things in mind: You can find the needle in the haystack if you keep on looking for it because it *is* there.

Go-getter gets to go to China

*Perth Amboy resident
uses Web for Beijing job*

ELIAS
HOLTZMAN

Upon completion of this chapter I found several emails I had saved from my managers and colleagues who received the email. Here are a few of the heartwarming responses I received:

"You should be very proud of yourself Apara. It has been an honor knowing you and I always have admired your spirit and confidence. Never let anyone take that away from you."

"Good luck with following your dreams and I know you will be successful. Your determination and dreams have gotten you this far. You can do it."

"Not many people reach their dreams; you're a lucky woman to have done so. Nor are you the shy quiet girl everyone thought you were. You're definitely a go-getter. Good for you! Now go get them in training!"

"Good luck. It was a pleasure working with you. Even though we started off a little rough, we did smooth things out and you became one of my favorite people to work with. You were always attentive and conscientious of my department and its challenges. As you stated, this is not goodbye but see you later."

"You are so right about how you never know when one's paths may cross again. I truly hope ours will. I am much older than you and you are a little quirky like me but this is our charm and what made me like you for the person that you are."

"Thank you for always being so honest and generous with your advice and giving me encouragement back when I needed it the most."

"And so your story continues…..I feel fortunate that our paths have crossed. I want to thank you for your commitment to our clients and our team."

"That MADE ME CRY – I WISH YOU THE BEST OF LUCK WITH EVERYTHING"

After leaving this particular company I worked in New York for several month until the economy crashed in 2008. Social media was becoming big during this time and I was able to connect with many people who touched my life including even my former students from China.

In 2007, one of my Chinese students, Eric, came to New York on a business trip and contacted me. One October day in 2007 we met in Times Square after six years and I gave him a big hug. That weekend was Halloween and I was having a party at my home. Eric came and we had a wonderful time where he got to see my world in the USA and meet my friends.

Life is a beautiful mystery, especially where people are concerned. The world is very small and you never know when and where you will cross paths with someone again but, ultimately, you will.

Eric and I, Halloween 2007

Chapter 9

Miss Education

My time in China is still, to this day, the best two years of my life.

When I arrived in China for my first teaching year, the first two or three weeks on the campus of the Beijing Second Foreign Language Institute or "Er Wai" (in Chinese) were spent in a student dorm room as the housing for the "Foreign Expert Teachers" was not yet completed.

My arrival in China and my first night in my dorm room was a memorable one. I remember it was a hot and humid night. There was a loud floor fan in my room which I had no choice but to keep on as the room had no air conditioning. As the hot water was turned on only a few hours a day my shower water was ice cold. Before going to bed I spied a cockroach under the bed.

When I woke up the next morning with the sun streaming into my room and realized I was in Beijing and waking up to my dream come true I was happy, cockroach and all.

I was assigned to teaching a Freshman oral English class and a Sophomore reading class. All of my students spoke English but they needed to improve upon what they already knew.

I was 23, not much older than the students I was assigned to teach yet all of my students granted me to utmost respect and that was all that mattered.

Each teacher had to be assigned a Chinese name for paperwork purposes. I was given my Chinese name by the head of the foreign teachers. The name he gave me was Ma Ay Li. "Ma" because it sounded like Mahal, my maiden name, and "Ay Li" which means beautiful love. Yes, the man who christened me Ma Ay Li was blushing when he told me the English translation of my "new" name.

My students simply referred to me as Miss Apara.

My Master's degree secured me my position at this university. Beyond that I had no clue about lesson plans or how to actually teach. All I knew was that I had to somehow teach. When it was time for the semester to begin, for my oral English class I was handed a worn softcover textbook ten years out of date and was told "teach." Somehow I managed to get through that first year.

I was a fair teacher but a firm one too. One of my classes started at 2pm which was right after lunch and afternoon siesta time. One day all of my female students were in class but my handful of male students were missing. I closed my classroom door and waited well past the 2pm start time until there was a tiny knock on the door. When I opened to door all of my male students were standing there with sheepish grins on their faces. They thought they would just enter the classroom and take their seats but Miss Apara was having none of that.

I had all my male students stand in front of the classroom and I asked each of them why they were late. I needed to do this because had I been a Chinese teacher this would never have happened. Each student said the same thing; they had overslept. I asked them if they had alarm clocks and they all responded no. I volunteered to go and buy them all alarm clocks after class which they vehemently opposed as they would then be "losing face" in my eyes, the Chinese term for dishonor. After this one class none of my male students were ever late again.

In each class my colleagues and I always had a group of "special students" sitting in the very back rows. Special students were those who did not pass the college entrance exam. They were permitted to attend classes but as they would never attain a degree the Chinese teachers never paid much attention to them. I treated all my students equally and ensured the special students participated in my lessons just like the other students.

I had a special student named Mike in one of my classes. Mike was especially bright and a pleasure to have in class. All of a sudden Mike stopped coming to class. I ran into him one day on campus and simply told him that I missed having him in my class. After that encounter Mike never missed a class again.

Teaching for a second year at Er Wai proved to be more fruitful. When I went home to the USA for summer break I gathered plenty of books and articles to use in all of my classes.

My second year at Er Wei is when I actually became a good teacher.

During my second year my sophomore students were complaining about my boring lessons. I decided to turn the tables on them and said, "Ok, if you don't like the way I teach, you're going to teach the class." I put my students into groups. Each had to pick out an article, show it to me for approval, and teach the article to their classmates, the contents of which they would be graded on during final exams. When it came time for my students to teach their assignments I was just blown away by their creativity and work put into their projects. I believe all of them got A's on their final exam and I couldn't have been more proud of them.

My second year at Er Wai I created a peer-to-peer tutoring program for my oral English Freshman class. I paired the weaker students from this class with my stronger students from my now Sophomore class. All the students enjoyed working with each other and all passed their oral exams with flying colors.

When I was leaving China for good, one of my classes, Tourism Management Class I, made a photo album of themselves and gave it to me as a gift. On the inside cover one student named Vivian drew an exquisite pencil sketch of me. Other students provided photos of themselves and wrote captions under their photos.

"Thank you for your kindness. We will always love you!"

"You are the first and only teacher I've met that treats students on equal terms. I like you. Best Wishes"

"You did a good job as a teacher. You are easygoing, lenient and charming."

"I will always remember you."

These were not just fleeting empty sentiments. The Chinese are known for having long lasting memories. I know I made a lasting impression and difference.

Was I a good teacher? Did I leave my mark on my students?

I'm proud to say that yes, I did.

I wrote the following short story while living in

Beijing which was actually published in a book in China called <u>A Foreign Scholar's Perspective on China</u>.

"Culinary China-A Comical Critique"

All of my life, I've had this fascination with China. To me, it was a land of the exotic, full of mystery and new adventures waiting to be discovered. From an early age, I aspired to one day journey from my homeland of the United States to this mysterious land of over one billion people and see for myself what it was all about. My dream of visiting this magical land came in June of 1997 when I had the opportunity to come to Beijing as a tourist. I can still remember the first morning as if it were yesterday: I was standing at the entrance of my hotel, observing the city for the first time in daylight. It was early morning, the sun was shining bright, and it was turning out to be another one of Beijing's sultry summer days. Even at that early hour, the street was full of life. Bicycles were streaming past in an endless procession of people on their way to do their daily business. Cars were whizzing past, occasionally blowing their horns for passersby to beware. Street vendors were peddling their wares, and people walked by the hotel oblivious to the world around them.

For Beijing people, this was just another ordinary

morning. For me however, it was the day that would change my life. Standing there, I felt a sense of belonging come over me. It felt like I was home. From that moment, I knew that my dream of coming to China was more than just a dream; it was my destiny. From that moment also a new dream emerged; the dream of living in China.

After returning to the United States, my second dream became a reality one month later when I was hired to be a Foreign Expert teacher at the Beijing Second Foreign Language Institute. Without a moment's hesitation, I packed my bags, said my goodbyes to my family and friends, and off I went to begin a new life and career.

Now, I should explain one thing. Before coming to China, I was virtually ignorant about Chinese culture. I never studied Chinese History, didn't really know any Chinese people, and the only language I ever studied was Spanish. I can say that I was a big fan of Gong Li (famous Chinese actress) movies, but I don't know if this really makes a difference.

Children in the United States like to play in their backyards, and playing in the dirt is especially fun for a child. A familiar expression heard by many mothers upon seeing their children digging holes in their beloved flower gardens is "If you keep on digging, you're going to reach China!" Wow! Could this actually be possible? I don't think any child was ever brave enough to try and find out. In most cases, this statement was enough to get the child back into the house, and spare mom's flowers from an untimely death.

Children all the world 'round are always fussy eaters. American children aren't any different. No matter what a poor mother may do to tempt their child's palate, the child will usually find some reason or other not to eat the food mom has prepared. Trying to use guilt as a last resort to get proper nutrition into their child's body, many a frustrated mother will ultimately say "You'd better eat your vegetables. Don't you know there are starving children in China?" Sometimes, this statement worked. Other times, the child won the battle and got a meal they would willingly eat: A peanut butter and jelly sandwich (a favorite food of American children).

Lastly, children love animals. Many families are not complete without having a dog or a cat as part of their household. Virtually anything with a furry face and a cute expression is sure to bring a smile to any child's face. Sometimes though, this smile would turn into a frown when someone may say "Did you know that in China, they eat everything with four legs except a table?" Maybe the person saying this only wanted to make the child appreciate animals and stop pulling their poor dog or cat's tail. But, to a child, hearing this bit of information was almost as traumatic as having to eat all their vegetables at dinner (which, by the way, taste nothing like peanut butter and jelly sandwiches).

As I said earlier, we only find out what is myth when we grow up. Some adults may still be wondering if all the things they heard about China as a child are true or not. Some may never know. I, however, have had the privilege of coming to China and finding out myth from fact for myself. Well, I didn't need to come to China to find out that you will NOT reach China by digging a hole deep enough in your mother's flower garden. Science and Geography class taught me this. As I was never good at either subject, I forgot what you will actually find if you keep digging deeper and deeper, but I know it's definitely not China.

Starving children in China was yet another myth which I soon realized upon my arrival here. Everywhere you look, a restaurant is staring you in the face. From Sichuan to Cantonese style food, Muslim barbecue to Mongolian hotpot, the varieties are never ending. It seems as if there's one restaurant for every one person in Beijing. I wonder sometimes how they all manage to stay in business. I stopped wondering if there were starving children here. It seemed virtually impossible.

In fact, the Chinese adore food. I was amazed at the length of the menus of the restaurants I frequented. Page after page of endless delicacies to choose from. Even if I remained in China for the rest of my life, I don't think I could ever try them all.

Presentation of food is another thing the Chinese

take pleasure in. Steaming dishes come out looking colorful, fresh, and have smells which make your mouth water. Garnish a dish with a flower delicately made from a radish or carrot and all is complete. You don't have to wait long for your food to come either. Within minutes of the waitress taking your order, your food is on the table, waiting to be tasted.

I knew Chinese food in the United States was "Americanized," and not truly authentic to the taste. I wasn't sure though what "China" Chinese food would taste like, or even if I would like it. I'm pleased to say, it exceeded all my expectations.

Americans, on the other hand, are fairly basic when it comes to their food. Beef, pork, chicken, and fish are pretty much the only once living creatures you'll find on the menu of your favorite restaurant. Americans also eat the very basic parts of an animal's body, mainly the torso of the animal with the bones and the fat nicely taken out. Serve it with some mashed potatoes on the side, and you'll have a meal which will make any American happy. As far as the "leftover" parts of the animal's body go, mainly the organs, they just get made into pet food (as per my father, whose company happens to make pet food). But, China is not the United States.

I soon found out that the third myth about China which I learned as a child was indeed not a myth at all, but a fact. My mother was right; the Chinese do eat everything with four legs except a table! It didn't take me long to figure this out either.

Yes, there was beef, pork, and chicken on the menu. In addition, you could also find pig ear as a cold appetizer, sheep intestines, dog, even donkey, as well as a host of other dishes unheard of in America. I first learned what "tripe" meant when it was served in front of me. Stomach. Needless to stay, I stayed away from it.

Now, I really am an adventurous type of person. If I wasn't, I would never be in China. But, there are some lines of adventure I'm just not willing to cross. As a general rule, I won't stray far from beef, pork, or chicken. Specifically, I should say I only eat the parts of these animals which I can clearly recognize. Beyond that, I'll leave the adventure to someone else.

The Chinese have an interesting philosophy when it comes to their diet. They believe that to eat a certain part of an animal's body will be beneficial to the same part of your body. They believe to eat the intestine of a sheep will be good for your own intestines, to eat the heart of a duck will be good for your own heart, and so on. I'm open minded when it comes to new philosophies, but I'm closed-minded when it comes to what I put into my mouth. Maybe I should just say I'm closed-mouthed.

However, I became very vocal one day the second month I was in Beijing. On my way to a local grocery store,

I spotted a sorrowful little kitten outside a restaurant, in a cage. If I didn't believe what was said about the Chinese eating anything with four legs except a table before, I definitely was a believer now. To make a long story short, I now have a beautiful cat as a companion in my apartment. I know I can't save every poor furry animal that I may come across, but at least I saved one. Luckily, to this day I've never seen a dog or a cat anywhere near a restaurant ever since. If I had, I might be the only person in Beijing to have an indoor zoo, so to speak.

Once, when I was in Guizhou province, I was served dog soup. Luckily, soup is served at the end of a meal in China. So, all I had to do was politely excuse myself claiming I was ill from travelling. I just barely made it to the bathroom.

I know that when you're in a different culture, you do have to adapt yourself to that particular culture as much as you can. However, there are just certain things I cannot adapt to as an American. In the United States, dogs and cats are considered to be not only pets, but a member of the family. To me, eating one of these creatures would be the same as eating a relative. I simply cannot do it.

I should also admit that I was one of those fussy eater type of children. One thing I detest to this day is any type of seafood. I never liked it as a child, and I continue to dislike it as an adult. China, however, is not the place to dislike seafood.

Before I go on, one thing the Chinese are noted for is the lavish banquets they serve, complete with endless dishes of food. I should also say that it is considered impolite to not at least try a small portion of every dish when you're attending a banquet.

What is always served in abundance at these banquets is seafood. A lot of seafood. I never wanted to insult my Chinese hosts by saying I disliked what was served, but it left me in a dilemma as to how to avoid eating the seafood. This was quickly solved by me politely saying that I am allergic to it. This small lie worked, and I've managed to almost avoid seafood ever since.

It's a pity I don't like seafood, because the seafood dishes are especially well presented. Fish dishes are the most interesting to look at-served whole and generally decorated with an array of colorful fruits. Some Westerners don't like to look at a whole fish because they claim "The fish is staring at me", but this minor detail never bothered me. Keeping to the philosophy of eating certain parts of the body for good health, the Chinese will generally consume every part of the fish, including the tail. This is something I still don't understand. Humans don't have tails, so what good would eating the tail of the fish do? I haven't seen any Chinese persons with aquatic body parts yet, so I guess it can't do any harm.

Well, when you're in a different culture, I you're not expected to understand everything.

As I've said, my lie about being allergic to seafood has almost worked well. But, a person cannot possibly be allergic to everything. I found this out when I went to Inner Mongolia for a short vacation.

I travelled there with a good friend of mine to visit her family on China's National Day holiday. While in Inner Mongolia, I was welcomed warmly as a "new addition" to the family. I was a bit nervous about what types of food I might encounter, but nothing out of the ordinary crossed my mouth. As the days went on, I became more at ease.

Then, two nights before we were to depart, I was taken out to dinner by some friends of the family because I was a "special" guest. When you are considered a "special" guest in China, then you're obligated to try every single dish, and all eyes are on you to make sure you do. I was crossing my fingers that the meal would go along smoothly. It almost did.

At one point, I spied a bottle of Chinese liquor on the table. I asked my friend if it was a special liquor of Inner Mongolia. She replied "Yes, and you drink it with turtle blood." Turtle blood? I asked my friend "Where are we getting turtle blood from?" Soon after I asked, a huge bowl of turtle soup came out, with a glass of blood following. I now knew where the turtle blood was coming from.

Now, I was in a dilemma again. Turtle is not beef,

pork, or chicken; it comes from the sea. Seafood! I could not refuse, because I was the "special" guest. So, I had to try a bit. Basically, I put a little in my mouth and swallowed without chewing. This trick is something you learn as a child when your mother is forcing you to eat something you don't want.

Then came the blood.

Shots were poured, and a toast was made in my honor. I took a sip, and tried not to think about what I was drinking. Luckily, the drink just tasted like any ordinary Chinese liquor. This didn't matter much to me, because I knew I was drinking more than just liquor. My face must have been flushed, because people commented on how red it was. All I could say was, "Well, I drank turtle blood, so now my blood is good." What else could I say?

Luckily, I returned to Beijing in good health, which was a blessing since I had been ill during most of my trip. Maybe it was the turtle blood that aided in my recovery. But, I'm not going to switch to blood to cure my ailments from now on. Antibiotics suit me just fine.

After all this, I could just simplify my life and become a vegetarian. However, I've just decided to become a bit more creative. Rather than saying I'm allergic to seafood, from now I'm just going to say I'm allergic to banquets. That will solve all of my seafood problems, and it will keep me away from the Maotai (Chinese liquor) as well.

I've decided I don't want to be "special" anymore either. I'd much rather be just another ordinary commoner. Maybe then I'll be taken to McDonald's. Finally, I've decided to say that it's against my religious beliefs to let anyone order food for me. No one will question beliefs based on a higher authority.

Or, maybe I should just stick to eating at home..

Chapter 10

SoulCat

There is nothing mentioned in the "rulebook of life" which says a soulmate cannot be an animal. As animal lovers know all animals are special. However, at some point in your life you may come across that one special little animal that creeps into your heart and soul and becomes a part of you. For me it was a SoulCat named Zhang Miao or "Zhangy" as he was lovingly called.

People gravitate towards animals because they give unconditional love. Animal affection may very well be the purest form of love there is just for the simple fact that animals do not have human speech capabilities. Animals cannot state conditions.

With an animal, such as a cat, the love is felt when the animal is near you. To pet the smooth sleek fur of a cat produces a calming affect similar to rubbing the smooth "worry stones" of spirituality. Unconsciously the repeated stroking of a cat calms. As a response to the stroking the cat will begin to purr in a steady rhythm which, if listened to steadily, produces a trance, almost like listening to the repetitive crash of ocean waves on my sound machine. When a cat is snuggled close to you, you can feel its body warmth and it may also look at you and gently start licking your hand. Relaxation, a cat will only snuggle close to you if they trust you.

There are no worries. There is a calming effect. There is warmth…all without words.

I saved Zhangy's life when I was living in Beijing, PRC in 1997. At that time I thought of writing a book which I wanted to title *Beijing Diaries: Stories On Living A Red Life*. I never got around to writing that particular book but how Zhangy came into my life is mentioned in a short story I wrote back in 1998 called "How Dinner Became A Love Story."

Zhangy was a lovely cat. He had soft fur which was the same orange cream hue as a ginger snap cookie. Underneath his chin he had a solid orange strip which gave the appearance as if he were wearing a mask. He was a bit on the chubby side which made him easy to hug and cuddle.

Though Zhangy was his nickname I had a plethora of other nicknames for my dear little boy:

Zhang-a-Doodle

My beautiful, beautiful, beautiful boy

Buddha cat

Orange Baby

Baby Zhang

Lumpy kitty

This Boy

Zhangy was the first cat I ever cared for on my own. I never had the desire to have children of my own so Zhangy became my little baby and my best friend.

We used to play a wonderful game called Ears, no Ears! I would look at Zhangy with his ears pointed towards me and say "Ears!" Then, I would cover up his ears with my hands and say "No Ears!" When I removed my hand I would say "Ears!" once again. This game could go on for several minutes with Zhangy sitting nicely on my lap enjoying his mama's little game.

When I lived in China my apartment floors were smooth cement. When Zhangy was a young cat a game we played was I would gently push him across the floor where he would slide. Once he got up he would walk over to me so that I could slide him across again. Zhangy loved this game the most.

There were so many simple little things my Zhangy loved. Laying in the warm sunshine (Mr. Sunbeam, as I called the ray). Roasting up against the fireplace in winter. Hiding under my living room curtains. Crawling into the "tunnel" my bent legs made when I covered them with a blanket while lying on the sofa. Sitting on my bed and laying under the covers on my bed so that all you would see was a lump. Sleeping in the laundry room on top of my dry cleaning clothes or bedsheets which were spread out on the floor. Lastly, sleeping inside my bedroom closet where I occasionally forgot he was there and locked him inside. Same for a cabinet I have from Germany which he always tried to get into whenever it was open, I know Zhangy always forgave me for my errors as I am only human.

Whenever a guest and I were sitting on the sofa Zhangy would jump up and sit in between me and whomever else was on the sofa. When he got older and couldn't jump high anymore he meowed to be lifted up onto the sofa.

Over the years I acquired two other cats; Polly from Germany and Boo Boo from the vet Dr. Jan. Towards the other cats Zhangy exhibited kindness as best as a cat could. He always let Polly and Boo Boo eat first before he ate, even when I served his favorite food Ocean Whitefish Tuna. He was a good big brother.

When Zhangy was about eleven years old he developed a condition called Feline Hepatic Lipidosis (fatty liver disease). He stopped eating and became jaundiced. The veterinarian, Dr. Jan, had to insert a feeding tube where for several weeks I fed him medicine and food through the tube several times a day. It was very touch-and-go for a while and Dr. Jan was not certain Zhangy would pull through but he did. During this time, in 2008, I was unemployed and unhappy but in hindsight it was a blessing in disguise as no one would have been able to care for Zhangy as I did. Zhangy recovered from this ordeal and I had him in my life for almost another two full years.

As a thank you to Dr. Jan and everyone in her practice Zhangy "wrote" a story about his illness and recovery called "Mama's Bed."

I met my husband Johnny in 2010 and he got to know Zhangy for a good six month until, maybe, Zhangy realized that his mama found her SoulMan and it was ok for him to leave me.

In September 2010 Zhangy went into kidney failure and on September 28, 2010 I made the decision to have the final act of love administered to him, as euthanasia is referred to in the animal world.

Just as I got to say goodbye to my dear grandfather, I also got to say goodbye to my dear little SoulCat. Johnny and I went to the veterinarian's office for our final goodbye. I brought a bag of treats with me and fed them to Zhangy one by one. He so happily gobbled them up and I bitterly cried.

I just couldn't bring myself to hold him while he was put to sleep but at least I know that, whatever heaven he was going to, he was going there with a full tummy of his favorite treats.

Zhang Miao was a special little boy so he deserves his own chapter. I miss him every day and cry for him, good and happy tears, because he gave me thirteen years of nothing but happiness and joy.

"How Dinner Became A Love Story"

There is a saying in the United States which proclaims the dog to be man's best friend. Firstly, I am a woman, so immediately I am excused from the norm. Secondly, all my life I have had a particular affinity towards members of the feline species, so again I beg to be pardoned. Lastly, I'm not a dog person.

It's as simple as that.

Being the adventurous type, I decided to try my luck at working in China, Beijing to be specific. Moving to Beijing, as I so boldly did, involved some sacrifices, as many things in life do. One of these sacrifices was the separation from my beloved cat Maggie. Now, Maggie never showed her love for me in a conventional cat way. The occasional bite and swat of her razor sharp claws was substituted for purring and sitting on my lap. Still she was mine. I loved her, faults and all. All of us have our faults, don't we? But, I had to follow my dreams of going to China. So, left in the capable hands of my parents, we sadly parted. Well, I was sad. Maggie was indifferent. She was never one to be good at goodbyes.

After getting adjusted to living in my new world, I began to long for some companionship as I was living alone. Another human was out of the question. Humans are too complex sometimes. In China, man's best friend quickly becomes man's best entree, and you already know my opinion of dogs. I once relented and bought lovebirds, but they died within 24 hours of each other (no reflection on my own love life). A cat crossed my mind a few times, but I just told myself no. So, I remained companionless.

For those of you who aren't familiar with Beijing life, food is a major part of the culture. Remember when your mother told you to finish your brussel sprouts because there were starving children in China? Well, with restaurants coming out of your ears from all angles, I can hardly see how this could ever be possible. I still wonder how they all manage to stay in business.

Restaurants in Beijing don't make a big issue of trying to attract customers as they sometimes do in the USA. In a land of one billion people, a restaurant going out of business is about as likely as Elvis losing his title as King of Rock and Roll. However, some restaurants do make a point of displaying their menu items in a live, visual form outside. A common sight is cages stuffed with chickens that look like survivors of war, fish in tanks that look like the losers of the war with the chickens, and some other displays as well. Nothing out of the ordinary to an American's tastebuds. But, keep in mind my comment about man's best entree...

On one of my ventures out to our Chinese version of ShopRite, I spied something very out of the ordinary outside a local restaurant. To my horror, above a cage of chickens from a recent war sat a kitten which was obviously that evening's blue plate special. It was a sorrowful sight to see; No water, a measly chicken bone to pick on, and totally trapped.

Now, all of you know how I feel about cats. Well, what happened next could've come straight out of a supermarket romance novel: The kitten gazed at me with sorrowful, longing eyes. My heart skipped a beat, and I gazed back with mutual longing. It let out a pitiful meow. Then it happened. The moment we long for all our lives. It was love. So unexpected, so perfect, so right. That meow said it all. "Oh beautiful Goddess, save me from this wretched fate of mine. Take me, and my devotion will be yours forever"...

Ok, maybe the Goddess part is overdoing it just a bit. But, this is my story, so just keep on reading...

I was appalled at the sight, but I knew what had to be done. I had a mission. I raced home, made a couple of phone calls to get authorization to take on a roommate, gathered up all my hard earned cash, and off I went to the rescue, hoping the little soul wasn't already being served as the main course.

To my relief, the kitten was just as uncooked as I left it. I quickly summoned the waitress out, expressed my intentions in Chinese (which was as pitiful as the kitten), and for the cost of a true blue plate special ($6.25 to be exact), the kitten was mine. My soulmate. I bundled the kitten up in my jacket, and off we went into the sunset (well, darkness) to begin our new life together.

For those of you who aren't female, there's something you need to know about the female psyche. We have this thing called "female bonding." It's when a female feels this special connection with another female so much so that you could become inseparable and lifelong friends. I just knew the bonding thing was at work here. I thus named my new little girl Mimi.

My life was complete.

I had a gal pal. I had a companion. I had a cat!

Now, as all good mothers do, I took my new charge to the vet to have a checkup. Before I go on, one thing I should mention is that I am ignorant when it comes to anything other than human genitalia. Well, to my utter disbelief, the kindly Chinese vet informed me that I was the owner of a healthy MALE cat. Mimi a mister? What happened to female bonding? How could I be so wrong? Still in shock, I proceeded to take my new little boy home. A renaming ceremony was in order. Henceforth, Mimi was known as Zhang Miao.

Another lesson is in order here regarding names in China. The Chinese take much pride and care in picking a name for their child. Giving your child a name with a special, significant meaning reflects the life of the child, and sometimes their personal characteristics. Why did I choose Zhang Miao? My cat is Chinese, so giving him a Chinese name seemed appropriate. Zhang is a common surname in China. Miao is pronounced the same as meow. Simple enough.

Later on, my students informed me that the English translation for Zhang is paper. Well, I wouldn't say my little guy particularly likes paper. Objects which shatter and fly into a million pieces when swatted tickles his fancy more. Zhang Miao truly is a Chinese cat at heart. His love of the color red became apparent when he decorated my floor with red nail polish, bottle and all. Many a delicate trinket has been lost forever in his quests of curiosity. Whoever said that curiosity killed the cat must have been a former cat lover who owned a crystal shop. You can guess why I used the word "former." Fear not though, Zhang Miao is still among the living.

As I stated earlier, all of us have our faults.

Zhang Miao is now a year old. He has grown into a beautiful cat of orange color with warm yellow eyes. Still, he loves to test my patience. His cravings for attention at 6am compete with my cravings for sleep on most mornings. He's cleverly figured out that hitting my face with his paw would surely wake me up. He's learned that teeth are a useful weapon which he tries out on me most of the time, in the most loving ways. His quests for trying to break things never fail to emerge when I'm on an important phone call. Many an eardrum has been shattered from my deafening "Zhang Miao get down from there!"

This may not be your conventional love story, but love happens in all shapes and forms. I love Zhang Miao with all my heart. He's faithful. He gives me happiness. He is my friend. Isn't that what love is all about?

They say you can tell a lot about a person by looking into their eyes. This holds true for animals as well, even more. I see the terror when he's done something wrong. I pity the sadness as I leave for work, and I'm comforted by the joyful glimmer when I come home.

Sometimes, though not very often nowadays, I even detect a grateful look of thanks. Though we can't bond as females do, we are bonded in other ways nevertheless. He knows I'm responsible for his being alive, and he knows I'll always keep him safe from harm. I know he'll always be loyal to me. I couldn't ask any more from love. Could anyone?

One last thing about Zhang Miao... I taught him how to fetch!

"Mama's Bed"

My most favorite place to sleep in the whole world is on mama's bed. Even from the time when I was a little kitty I used to love sleeping on mama's bed all the time.

When I started to get real sick I didn't go on mama's bed anymore; I slept under the bed and didn't come out. As I can only meow but not speak, staying under the bed all day was the only way I knew how to let mama know that I was getting sick and I needed help. That's when mama took me to see you. I didn't like how you poked and prodded at me all the time – taking x-rays, ultrasounds and blood and I REALLY did not like it when you put that tubey thing in my neck and down my stomach. I tried to always be a good little boy and not give you any trouble. Even if I wanted to put up a fight I didn't know how; I was just too weak.

A few times when I was very, very sick and had that tubey thing in me mama picked me up and put me on the bed with her but I just jumped down and went under the bed to sleep. I know mama was sad and missed me because I sleep cuddled up next to her always. I'm lucky mama understands me well because I have been her little friend for so many years. Mama understood I was weak and sick and she also knew in her heart that when I am all better I will sleep on her bed again with her. Mama never told me this but I can understand mama just as well as she understands me so I just knew.

When you took that tubey thing out of me I knew I was all better. When mama brought me home she carried me upstairs and put me on her bed. I stayed on her bed and slept and slept and slept until I got hungry. I jumped off the bed to go eat but then I jumped right back up. Mama took a picture of me up on her bed:

For the first time in so very long I was up on mama's bed again and I stayed with mama on the bed the whole night purring cuddled up next to mama, just like always.

I really don't want to remember how very sick I was anymore but I'm remembering now for one last time only to say thank you to you for helping me get better.

Mama likes to write stories and she can write A LOT! Ten years ago she wrote a story about how she rescued me and how I was when I was little. Mama said I can give you this story about me to read since you didn't know me from when I was a very little kitty and because you saved my life. The story is on the next page.

Mama saved my life over 10 years ago when she rescued me from being eaten up at a restaurant in China. You saved my life from ending due to liver disease.

I know I have a lot of life left in me but what a lucky little boy I am to have had my life saved not once but twice in one lifetime!

Thank you and lots of love,

Zhang Miao (aka Zhangy)

Chapter 11

Off to Deutschland

I spent two years in China. In my second year I began a relationship with a man from Germany, the brother of my next door neighbor, whom I met when he was on vacation in China. Over time we got engaged and I decided that I would move to Germany to be with him. I moved to Beijing to pursue my dreams. I moved to Germany for love.

Though I was sad to leave China I felt it was my time and that I had contributed all that I could. I was excited to start my new life in Germany but sad to leave China and I cried the entire eight hour plane ride to Germany with my little Zhangy safely tucked under my seat in his carrier.

As I had no job to go to the first order of business was for me to enroll in German classes. I went from being teacher in one country to student in another. I enrolled in the Goethe Institut, a well-known German language school. My first class in Grundstufe Eins (German Level I) was quite memorable. The teacher started us off by introductions and she said directly to me "Ich heisse

Irmtraud." I knew "Ich heisse" meant "I am" but I had no idea what Irmtraud meant. It took me a few minutes to figure out that she was telling me her name. Slowly I got the hang of German though I was never proficient in the German grammatical structure. Most foreign language students, such as the Chinese, are hesitant to speak another language unless they can speak it to perfection. For me, as long as I could be understood and could understand that was all that mattered. Over time I developed my own level of fluency which I have retained to this day.

I lived in a beautiful university town called Goettingen. My fiancée was an anesthesiologist at the university hospital and his boss, Tom, happened to be an American. Tom told my fiancée there were several Americans living in Goettigen and they had formed a group called "Americans Abroad in Goettingen". This group met once a month at a local bar for a Stammtisch (informal meeting) and I was eager to attend and hopefully get some useful tips on living in Germany and make new friends.

Without shame I can tell you these Americans were the most miserable group of people I'd ever met in my life. Whereas I thought they would be eager to teach a newcomer the "ropes," all they did was complain about Germany. I remember clearly one woman telling me, "You have to choose between a job and your fiancée because you can't have both here." I left my first meeting beyond discouraged, yet I went back the following month.

Despite the negativity I kept going to monthly meetings hoping things would change and one time they did.

At the start of every meeting everyone introduced themselves by name, state they came from and what their profession was.

At one particular meeting I got tired of the "usual," especially people making the stereotypical New Jersey jokes once they found out that was where I was from. At this meeting I said, "My name is Apara. I come from New Jersey and I'm doing nothing."

It was at this meeting that a man named Milo was in attendance. His version of how we met is, "When I heard that I knew she was someone different from the rest." This is how Milo and I became friends.

Milo was the only one in the group who extended a true hand of friendship. We discovered that we lived close by and he offered to show me one of his favorite grocery stores. Milo became my friend, my brother and my rock. In chapter 12 my story "Angel Wings" was my gift to Milo when he decided to leave Germany and move back to the USA.

Not all was lost at these meetings. At one I met a man named Dave who taught English at the university and he hired me as a part time ESL instructor and he also secured a few private English tutoring students for me.

By my first year I had learned German, was working and everything was going well except for my relationship which had begun to unravel. My fiancé was a good man but we were clearly incompatible. We were living together but we didn't know what to do.

One time Milo came to our apartment and witnessed a heated argument between my fiancée and I. Milo sat the both of us down and said, "Have you two ever thought about being friends?" My fiancée and I both looked at each other. No, we never thought this but once we realized we could be friends everything changed between us as if a dark cloud was lifted. We have remained good friends to this day.

I needed to stand on my own feet and one day I saw a job advertised in a local newspaper seeking an English speaking account manager for a company that made hair color swatch books which can be found in hair salons. I applied, was interviewed and hired and the company even granted me the necessary work visa. As I was making a full time salary I was able to move out of my fiancée's apartment and rent one of my own.

Was the American woman correct who told me, "You have to choose between a job and your fiancée because you can't have both here?" I did have both; I had a job and a fiancée but we mutually chose to end our relationship so, in fact, I had my cake and ate it too.

I found another needle in the haystack and that made all the difference. Most importantly, this is a lesson on how not to let unwanted negativity affect your life. I made my time in Germany a success despite what others had to say.

There were a few Americans who worked at the university and had lunch together one per week. After I secured my full time job and apartment I joined them and let them know. After I told them my news it was as if you could cut the air with a knife. I wasn't trying to shove my success in their faces. Rather, I was trying to prove a point as to my resiliency; If you tell me I can't do something I will but only to prove it to myself and no one else.

I lived in Germany two years when I decided to move back to the USA as, after living abroad for four years, I missed my family and my friends.

This is a story I wrote while in Germany about a failed relationship. The wine glasses are real. I bought them when I lived in Germany and I think of my time in Germany fondly when I look at them. The wine glasses could signify any loss, a bad day or memory you hold on to or even a good memory, depending on how you look at the colors.

"The Wine Glasses"

I believe that when a person moves into a new home, the first thing that they
should buy is a set of wine glasses. Wine glasses bring luck, because they invite happiness into a new home. With wine glasses comes wine shared between friends during a wonderful meal of stories and laughter, a glass or two shared with a lover on a quiet evening listening to romantic music on the stereo, and a glass drunk alone just because you are happy and content remembering the memories shared between friends and lovers over a similar glass of wine in another time and place.

I was not in search of wine glasses when I stumbled upon the perfect ones. It was at a flea market, and there they were sparkling like gems, looking for someone to fill them up again. It was a set of four, the perfect number for a quiet dinner with friends, and more than enough for the times with someone special. Their bases and rims were outlined with a dull gold color, and swirls of this same colored gold decorated the place where you wrap around your hand. They were old, yet they shone new with the promise of many more glasses of wine to share.

Each glass had a different color. The first was green, like the first grass of springtime after a long cold winter. The second was a royal amethyst purple, and it could have been an amethyst if it took on a shape other than a glass. The third was blue, and to look at it was to see the warm Caribbean ocean beckoning all to enter and feel its warmth. The last was colored the rich red of passion and love. Maybe, to some, all these multicolored glasses wouldn't go together well with some expensive dinner set. But, not everyone can see the real value behind an object. Sometimes people see only what's on the surface, while others look on to see the world beyond the surface. When I looked at them, I did not see four mismatched colored wine glasses of old. I saw them being held as people were toasting in the new year many new years ago, wishing happiness to loved ones on Christmases past, at marriages meant to last a lifetime, and for the births of new generations...so many happy memories these glasses held, and they shone and laughed knowing that they still had much more happiness to give. So, I bought them, promising to give them new memories in addition to what they held onto from their past.

Afterwards, we met. It was pleasant enough yet not the same. The conversation was quiet at times because we didn't know what to say anymore, though before we could talk on forever. Before.

You gave me back a bag of my possessions, things which you packed away as to not remind yourself of me. In this bag was a bottle of wine-the wine we were supposed to share during a happy time. But, things change, and with those changes the hope for happy times becomes a memory.

The wine glasses now sit in my cabinet. When I open it, I can still see that they glow anew, but soon the dust will dull their shine, and wipe away their smiles. Maybe they'll hope to one day come out into the sunlight again, but then they'll realize that my promise was broken. There in my cabinet they will remain, with no more wine filling their brims. They'll become a memory too in time, but they can never bring back what the present has taken from them.

Chapter 12

Angel Wings Kaleidoscope

"One of the most beautiful qualities of true friendship is to understand and to be understood"

*- Lucius Annaeus
Seneca, Roman Philosopher*

One day I took a look at all of my friends on my social media site and I came up with this post to describe my world of friends or kaleidoscope as I called it:

Who makes up the facets of your kaleidoscope? Aside from the obvious friends, family and colleagues I have some pretty amazing ones in mine: a childhood pen pal from Australia, my Sophomore year high school friend from the Bahamas, friends who I met while living in China and Germany, friends who have dated famous rock stars, two actress friends, an amazing jazz singer friend, my 5th grade favorite grammar school teacher friend, a few pretty cool neighbor friends, the woman who married us and the musician who played at our wedding friends, friends Johnny graduated high school with, a cigar manufacturer and his wife friend, a sheriff's officer friend who I beat up in 8th grade and even a few friends who I've never met in person but like very much and hope to meet one day, just to name a few. I'm careful who I let into my kaleidoscope and I do feel blessed by those of you who I let in and for your friendship.

There are two friends especially, Tony and Robert, who changed the way I am and who led me to my true love, Johnny, just by who they were to me. Tony is still in my life, a friendship of nearly 25 years. Sadly, I lost touch with Robert many years ago. Robert lives on in my heart and Johnny has all of the qualities which made me love Robert, my first love

They say you never forget your first love. I can't imagine every single first love out there was memorable, but Robert certainly was. He was respectful, loving and kind especially considering he was quite a number of years older than me. The stages of life we were in were just too different.

When I was younger I used to occasionally write letters to the editor of my local newspaper which were published more often than not. At different times both a letter about Robert and about Tony were published.

Friends are a gift to be cherished. My story "Angel Wings" was a gift to another friend of mine names Milo who is the brother I never had. Milo and I became friends when I was living in Germany and he was my rock. When he was leaving Germany to move back to the USA I wrote "Angel Wings" as my gift to him for the gift of his friendship. Rather than perceive the story to be sad, it is in fact a permanent tribute to an amazing friend, a friend whose voice I heard in my car that fateful February night which changed everything; the voice that said "awake."

Not all of my friends know that I have Manic Bipolar but those I chose to tell, those friends closest to me, understand and support me. With any chemical imbalance it's important to have a strong support network. Even if you think you have no one, you have me. I understand exactly what you are going through.

In 2007 when I was going through yet another disappointing dating ordeal Tony wrote me the following email: "What are you sad about. You're smart, beautiful and lots of fun. It's not your problem some people don't get it."

Tony was right. I get it now.

If you feel you are friendless know that Robert and Tony are real persons and they exist. There are many Roberts and Tony's out there in the world, as well as a kaleidoscope of others you may not have met yet. You never know when you might walk around the corner and bump right into a friend, new or old. That is the beauty of life.

I am not a broken angel anymore. I have wings. I always have and within my wings are all of the friends in my life who are near and dear to me, near and dear to my heart.

Thank you Tony, Robert, all of my friends and Johnny, my best friend, most of all.

Tony will receive one of the first copies of my book and I hope my book makes it into Robert's hands one day too. I want him to know just how much he means to me to this day.

There are some people on this earth you only meet once in a lifetime, if you are lucky. One such person is Robert Vargas of Perth Amboy, whom I have the privilege of knowing.

Robert is a respiratory therapist at Raritan Bay Medical Center, Perth Amboy Division. Personally and professionally, I have never seen a more loving or caring person. He does his job to the best of his ability and with a smile. He puts people at ease, which makes a world of difference in a tense situation.

Even more personally, Robert has touched my life in a special way. He has always been there when I needed him. Just a few simple words would always cheer me up and make me happy when I needed it. He is a loyal friend in a class all his own. My life is all the better because he is a part of it, and there are just so many words to express my gratefulness to him.

Robert, if I haven't told you this lately, I think you're wonderful.

A.M.
TNT 1/21/92 Perth Amboy

Lucky to have him as a friend

TNT TUE. 10/16/90

I would like to tell everyone about a dear friend of mine, Anthony Santana Jr.

Tony is my best friend. He is a very caring person, and has always been there for me and lended both ears when I need them.

I consider myself a very lucky person to have a friend like Tony in my life. I'd like to take the time now to let him know how special he is to me.

Apara Mahal
Perth Amboy

NEIGHBORS

93

"Angel Wings"

Some people have angel wings which allow them to touch the sky and reach for the unreachable...to touch the limits of the sky and to go beyond where only faith and hope can lead you further.

I never had angel wings of my own. I had an angel.

He was the one to carry me up to the places I never thought I could reach. He brought me closer to the stars and to the love within. His wings were enough for the both of us to surpass the hardships. Before him, I never thought I needed wings. I'm a broken angel, and even if I had wings they wouldn't take me far. I didn't know what real angel wings were, nor could I ever imagine before the peace within those wings could bring.

When he came into my life, his wings were enough for me. He flew me to those places where I could feel the joys that are lost to those in the chaos of the ground. Together we went to the outer limits where only the love within was all that mattered.

Now, my angel is flying far away. With him he'll take his wings as he'll need them to surround him more than I will. I'll be left on the ground in the chaos. I'll be left to look up in the sky and to wonder if I'll ever touch the faces of the stars again. The stars were so beautiful when we were up there together. Their light shone so brightly that his wings even glowed. He always glowed. It made the chaos seem so insignificant and the love seem real and not some illusion that's on the ground.

What you've never felt the angel wings, your life is just a mass of confusion and shattered thoughts. But, to feel the angel wings is to have the strength to be fearless and feel safe within.

My angel wings will be gone. I'm afraid of never feeling their warmth and safety again. I'll be left standing on the ground in the chaos....looking up....always looking up..............and waiting for the day my angel wings will come back and fly me to the stars again.

I'm a broken angel. My wings belonged to someone else.

If I could have one wish, I would wish for angel wings. They wouldn't have to be as large and beautiful and his; they would just have to be strong enough to take me back to the stars.

The ground is a very cold place without the warmth of angel wings.

Chapter 13

A Sunny Day of Unemployment

I've been unemployed more time than I'd like to count and for long periods of time I wish not to remember. I wrote the story "Destination" in 2008 during a period of unemployment.

"Destination" is actually about an employed person but there is a moral to the story. It's also my first attempt ever at writing fiction.

During one period of unemployment in 2004 my friend and former director Margot wrote me the following email just after I had celebrated my birthday. I have this email hanging on my refrigerator, as a reminder to never forget:

"Dear Apara. Happy birthday to you and a wonderful new year with some of your dreams being fulfilled. I know that the previous year brought with it some major disappointments. Since 9/11 and having learned that my daughter would be dead had she gotten the job that she really really wanted, my philosophy on life has changed quite a bit. We never know whether a disappointment today might not lead to something tremendously good tomorrow. You are such a nice, intelligent, good person. Good things will come to you as they have, I am sure, in the past."

Margot was right. Everyone should have a Margot in their life. If you don't, you now have her words as well as mine to keep you going.

As long as you wake up breathing, no matter what your day will bring, it will be a sunny day of unemployment.

"Destination"

3:45am

Every day without fail my alarm clock wakes me out of a deep slumber. Most days I don't care but today, just before that blaring buzzer sounded, I dreamt that I was walking on a beach with the warm sun beaming down and the cool ocean water streaming gently over my feet. As I walked along the beach I came upon a very unusual looking seashell and at the very second I reached down to grab it my alarm clock sounded. I felt so peaceful and happy on the beach until the buzzing of my alarm clock brought me into reality – my reality - waking me up to a cold and dark bedroom with no sunlight.

A warm sunny day only exists in my dreams as the weather forecast for today is blustery with heavy rain predicted. As I lay in the darkness of my bedroom I can already hear the raindrops pelting hard against my apartment window and I dread the thought of having to go outside. For a moment, one brief moment, I almost close my eyes again hoping to transport myself back to that beach. Then I rise from my bed to get ready for my day. At 3:45am the countdown begins and I have no time to spare. My train leaves at 5:20am on the dot and I have to be on that train. My job depends on me catching that train on time.

I don't really like my job but I need some way to pay the bills that come without fail each month. There's nothing else out there for me and, besides, I've been doing the same job now for over ten years. With the economy getting worse I'm lucky that I have a job at all. Anyway, even if I wanted to, it's too late for me to do something else and I'd lose the benefits, pension, and all that other necessary good stuff we need for when we get old. A job is a job and I deal with what I have, like it or not.

When I was young and had real dreams, I used to crave excitement and stimulation. Now, I'm content with the mundane and the same routine day in and day out. Alarm clock sounds at 3:45am. I jump out of bed, take a shower, brush my teeth, get dressed, drink a quick cup of instant coffee and then I'm out the door and on my way to the station.

At exactly 5:20 am my train departs the station. I observe the people on my train as I do every day and I see the same people, the same self-absorption, the same day in and day out. There are many "suits" as I like to call them. Hundreds of suits boarding my train wearing neatly pressed dark business attire, crisp dress shirts and neat spotless ties. They juggle their morning paper in one hand and their blackberry in the other. It's rare that a suit makes eye contact with me but why should they? I am no one to them. The "skirts" aren't any better though the skits usually chat loudly with their girlfriends rather than reading the paper or looking at their blackberries. I don't exist to the skits either.

Occasionally I see families on my morning train; A mother and father in jeans with two happy kids going on some fun excursion. I don't know and I don't care where they are going though, when there is a warm sunny day, I do wish that it was me going off to some fun place instead of being stuck on my train.

Today is not a sunny day. It's cold on the train and everyone looks tired and miserable and I'm just doing my job like I do every day.

I see her today but she's there every day just like the rest of them. She sits in the same seat and always looks deep in her thoughts. Unlike them, she looks up at me as I pass by and smiles. My job doesn't require me to smile but something about her makes me smile back. She never speaks to me. She only smiles then looks away. I don't know why I smile back at her. Maybe it's just out of politeness because that's what I was taught growing up. When I am acknowledged I am always polite.

My job is a thankless one but I don't need thanks from anyone. I don't get paid to be thanked. I get paid to do my job. Besides, who bothers to say thank you to anyone anymore? I can't remember the last time even a store clerk thanked me for making a purchase in their store. People used to say "Thank You" and even "Have a Nice Day". No one seems to have nice days anymore and everyone is too consumed with their own lives to bother with being grateful to others.

When my train reaches its final stop she is the last passenger to get off. She walks up to me and I hear her voice for the first time:

"Today is my last day on your train. I'm going to move down South where the weather is nice and I can start my own business. I want to thank you for your warm smile each day. Your smile gave me something to look forward to each morning. Don't ever stop smiling."

In a moment she was gone; lost among the masses headed towards their final destination. I stood there on the platform reflecting on what she said to me. Then I got back on my train and my train left the station once again, just like it does every day.

Tomorrow my alarm clock will once again wake me up at 3:45am. I may not dream of a beach but I will wake up to a sunny day.

Chapter 14

The Boy and the Golden Egg

This is what my writing in mania was like. Picture a child on Easter Sunday in a vast field littered with a multitude of brightly colored Easter eggs. There is a contest, a race, going on to see who can collect the most plastic eggs. First prize is a huge delicious chocolate egg wrapped in shiny golden tinfoil. We'll call the prize the golden egg. This little child wants the golden egg badly. So with basket in hand, he goes forth eagerly into a vast field of brightly colored plastic eggs, trying to grab up as many as possible.

Little children lose focus very quickly. One moment he or she is fervently collecting eggs. Suddenly, a yellow butterfly comes into sight flitting around the field and the child drops his basket to stare in awe.

A moment later he realizes he's forgotten his egg collecting, so he quickly resumes his task at hand. Minutes later the boy spies an unusual colored rock on the ground, which he picks up to examine thus once again forgetting the race.

Does the boy win the race and the golden egg?

Yes he does!

All of his hard work and effort paid off in the end despite the occasional distractions.

How does this relate to writing in mania?

I am the boy. The contest is my idea for a short story or piece. The field is my computer keyboard. The plastic eggs are my words and thoughts. The golden egg was my completed short story written to absolute perfection.

Sometimes it would take just a few hours to achieve my golden egg. Once, it took all night.

The process to achieve my golden egg was a manic episode.

There is one slight differential between the boy and I: I was afraid.

Perhaps there is a phobia somewhere to describe my fear, but the fear was fear of losing my words. Phobias are irrational fears and surely loss of words sounds irrational, except for in a manic mind.

I know now that I wrote in manic episodes but, in the past, it was just the way I wrote.

An idea for a short story would enter my head and immediately I went to my computer to begin typing. The words would flow out of my fingertips, egg after egg after egg.

Manic episodes are characterized by loss of concentration and focus. I would switch off my thought flow to read something on the internet or perhaps go out and smoke. Nevertheless, these are the butterflies and rocks. In the race to win the golden egg, eventually time had to be called in order to count eggs and determine the winner.

In my race, there was no timekeeper. There was no time. I would spend hours upon hours typing away at my keyboard. Despite being tired I would push myself on. I was afraid if I stopped and resumed at a later time that all my perfect words, my beloved eggs, would not be there. This could go on for hours. This did go on, on occasion, all night without sleeping. I could only stop and rest when I had the golden egg, my idea of perfection.

Now I realize that nothing needs to be perfection. I know that there is no race. I am able to pace my writing, stop and go back whenever I want. It's a very liberating feeling. Every day I write I have to always tell myself there is no race. There is no race. There is no race. This is what brought my book to completion.

Chapter 15

Archives of My Life

"I have just created something totally illogical."

— *Field of Dreams*

No one said writing was easy. Writing while having to constantly monitor your protective shield is an even greater challenge.

When I began writing this book and compiling stories about my life, everything came to me in a rush; forty years in a rush, all at once. It was wonderful and good, until it wasn't.

Instead of egg hoarding, I was bubble-watching in my head. Imagine a little child with a bubble wand blowing bubble after bubble in the air. When you look up at the iridescent balls floating in the air you feel a sense of peace and calm. In reality bubbles pop and dissipate. In my mind my idea bubbles stayed floating around me without any "off" switch, the result being three virtually sleepless nights. Unlike a manic episode where I would have high energy after very little sleep, in this hypomanic (mini manic) episode I was tired but yet somehow I still functioned.

The problem was the beautiful ideas kept flowing and floating peacefully through my mind nonstop. I didn't have the compulsion to keep on writing as I knew, this time, that my ideas weren't going anywhere, but these happy ideas had no "off" switch, thus preventing me from sleeping and getting adequate rest. After three days of very little sleep, I was on the verge of my shield cracking. That's when I sought help and was admitted to a mental facility for ten days of, well, rest and treatment. Lesson learned. Hard lesson learned but it all turned out for the best. What I had was insomnia due to a hypomania (mini manic) episode. Luckily it wasn't any worse.

I called the facility "the home," which is a term the character Sophia Petrillo of the "Golden Girls" television show used to refer to the nursing home she had resided in. In "the home" I met wonderful people, both patients and staff alike, all of whom reminded me of various people in my life: friends and mentors. I got the chance to meet several people suffering from depression, the flip side of my demon.

I did too much too soon and tested the strength of my shield to the point where it almost cracked. I created a "sonic boom" in my head, which nearly exploded. Lucky for me, it didn't. I don't know moderation in words and writing; this is one of the things I have to learn.

I never attempted to write a book before. I suppose somewhere exists a formula or even an entire book explaining exactly what you are supposed to do. As I've always liked doing things my own way, this was no exception.

This is what writing in a hypomanic episode was like:

Imagine a row of baking pans on the counter. Each baking pan had a number assigned to it. Think of the number as the title of the chapter. Somehow chapter titles came easy. The content and words came easily too, just in a variety of idea spurts. The spurts can be likened to roman candles with bursts of sparks shooting off everywhere. Just when I'd move onto another pan, a roman candle would go off with a variety of ideas both for that pan and for others so I'd have to shuffle around pans inserting the "ingredients." Luckily, with technology, it wasn't as frantic as it sounds. Most days I'd have about four documents on my computer in addition to another folder where I can reference what is not already opened.

This may sound like a form of organized disorganized chaos. But it worked. I've never asked anyone who has written a book what their formula for writing and organization is. Do they work on and complete one chapter first before moving on? I don't really care since my own way worked out fine.

I couldn't help but imagine what it would have been like writing this book in a true manic episode. The single word which comes to mind: terrifying. I don't want to imagine and cannot imagine what could have happened.

In mania focus isn't there. You cannot train yourself to focus because it's out of your control.

Here's something humorous:

They say people with mania should reduce stress in their lives. I work in a hospital emergency room and on a rescue squad, and I'm perfectly fine. Start writing a book and I end up in a mental treatment facility.

Go figure! Well, I never said I was normal and, apparently, neither is my mind.

I was tempted to title this chapter Medicated Maniac. Why Medicated Maniac? Who else but a maniac ends up in a mental treatment facility for ten days for treatment of insomnia due to creative ideas floating through their head peacefully but with no off switch? Yours truly of course! I had to re-battle a hypomanic episode in the early stages of writing this book, which I thankfully overcame with a slight medication adjustment.

Lithium is not a cure-all; it's a protective shield that is capable of cracking if pushed too hard. What pushes my shield to the point of cracking is creative writing and creative writing alone. Crazy, isn't it?

I still have to work on training myself to focus, just in a different way. I find that I get bored in my own solitude of writing, so occasionally I need to get up from my chair, walk around, read the news on the internet, and then resume my writing. These actions are controlled, deliberate and necessary.

Why did this hypomanic episode happen to me?

I Forgot There Was Never Any Race.

Chapter 16

Blankets and Pillows

During my undergraduate and graduate school days, I worked in the admitting and emergency room registration departments of a local hospital. I enjoyed helping people, but I didn't know what type of career I could have in a hospital environment. I was never good in math or science, so becoming a doctor or a nurse was out of the question.

Right after graduate school, my life took a drastic turn when I got the opportunity to teach in China for two years, and from there I moved to Germany for two more years before moving permanently back to the United States. In the United States I held a few corporate jobs and several periods of unemployment. I wanted direction, but direction never seemed to come my way. My father always said what I needed to find was a mentor but a mentor, like direction, just never came.

Fast forward twelve years later. I was unemployed once again during an economic depression and desperate to find any sort of work, even part time. This was hard to do given my vast experience and over qualifications. I then decided to revert back to what I knew: emergency room registration. One hospital I happened to apply to did not require a resume, only a short description of my qualifications.

They say things happen for a reason. Exactly one year to the day of applying for the position of emergency room registrar at a particular hospital – and exactly one week after being released from the mental facility after my accident – I got called to interview at this hospital, and the rest is history.

I worked for four and a half years in the emergency room of a large hospital. My job was to register patients. I went from bed to bed collecting personal and insurance data and having them sign the customary consent forms. I was grateful to have a job after a significant period of unemployment.

My position was an hourly, clerical position and a far cry from the corporate salary I used to make. Some may have called this a step backward thirteen years. I thought so too for a while until I fully embraced my role and realized my life had come full circle, and after all I had been through I had the chance to begin again.

I love working in the emergency room because it gives me the opportunity to help people. Beyond collecting their personal information and insurance, I get them blankets and pillows and anything else I need to make them comfortable. When I look at the patients and their loved ones, I see myself and my loved ones. Most importantly, I see humans everywhere deserving of comfort, dignity and respect. Each time I'm there I see the faces of humanity.

I need to explain something about giving patient pillows, because it's not as easy as it seems. Pillows come shrink wrapped three in a plastic package. Once the package is opened, the individual pillows are wrapped with a crinkly plastic cover, which I remove. Some people leave this cover on, which I attribute to laziness and not thinking who would ever want to rest their head on a pillow and hear a crinkle sound. Once the crinkle cover is off, I slip the pillow into a crisp clean pillow case and bring it to the patient, where I gently place it under their head. If they want a blanket, I will tuck them in, making sure any appendage that could feel cold is covered.

Once a medical student asked where he could get pillows and blankets. I promised to show him only if he followed my method, which he agreed to. When he mentioned his patient was cold I showed him exactly where the blanket warmers were. The student was very appreciative of my teaching. I know he will make a fine, compassionate doctor one day.

Not everyone who comes in the emergency room will be healed, and death is a part of life. When the most critical patients come through the ambulance bay doors, I make sure to say a silent prayer of healing for them, especially the cardiac patients as the heart is the most precious organ of all.

Once a man came in with cardiac arrest, meaning his heart stopped. The paramedics handed me his driver's license so I could enter his information into our system. I stared at his license picture for quite some time. He had gentle eyes and a kind face. I prayed for his health. I thought his life had been lost, but then I learned he was revived. I'm not saying I produced a miracle, but a little prayer maybe went a long way.

Giving a patient a blanket and pillow and ensuring their comfort is what makes a good day.

Chapter 17

True Love: The Power of Coffee

"Love is real Apara. Don't sell yourself short. It will find you. And when it does, it will take you by surprise and knock you off your feet."

-Email from a friend, 2008

The word love is often misused, misguided, misinterpreted and often times purely conditional or fraught with some form of barter attached, except for true love.

Author Robert Fulghum once sat in a coffee shop in Seattle with a sign that read "Tell me a short love story and I will buy you coffee and make you famous." From all the stories people told him his book *True Love* was born. I will now tell you my true love story which also involves coffee.

I live in a tiny town which some affectionately call Mayberry. It's one of those Anytown USA places where you can walk the streets and people know you by name. Our municipal building is a tiny house and city hall is a trailer parked next to it. Main Street USA is littered with tiny shops to fill your every need and the town is surrounded by a vibrant canal. It's a lovely place to live.

There once was a small deli in Anytown USA called Jimmy's Deli. I started to frequent Jimmy's Deli in 2009 when I was unemployed. I'd sit and drink my morning cup of coffee and hang out with the "boys club;" a group of local men who also frequented the deli each morning.

It was in Jimmy's Deli where love found me and I didn't even know it. One day he walked through the door. He was rugged and handsome with hazel eyes and a tough exterior. His name was Johnny. He would walk into the deli to buy his morning paper where he would sit and read it with a cup of coffee not even glancing my way. I was smitten. Johnny usually only came into Jimmy's Deli on the weekends and I used to look forward to Saturday mornings.

One day during a snowstorm I walked into Jimmy's Deli and Johnny wasn't there. I asked one of the guys where he was and the man responded, "He's probably snow plowing his mother's driveway. He takes care of her driveway and the driveways of the other elderly neighbors."

A man who loves and takes care of his mother. Johnny's true character shined through. That was the moment I fell in love with him.

How I convinced Johnny that I was the woman he was destined to be with is another story. There is no formula on how love works and sometimes you just have to work on the one you love. Johnny didn't want anything to do with me so I had to figure out a clever way to get him to notice me.

I decided Johnny needed to get to know the real me so I started sending him the short stories I had written up to that point, all of the stories I've included in this book. I would send him one story per week. Whenever I saw him at Jimmy's Deli he wouldn't say a word.

One day someone told me Johnny was at the local bar and restaurant. I quickly got dressed and went there. He wasn't happy at first but then we got to talking and talked for hours. The rest is history.

Before I started to write this chapter I asked Johnny what I should write about him. He responded:

"Johnny is the greatest person I ever met in my life."

He's right. Actually, Johnny was once destined for greatness. He played baseball from childhood and was good and fast. Johnny was a local legend and all the kids looked up to him. He made it as far up to the minor leagues where a shoulder injury ended his baseball career.

Had Johnny not injured his shoulder I wouldn't be surprised if he made it into the Cooperstown Hall of Fame one day. Lucky for me, for us, he did not or we wouldn't be together today.

Johnny is a simple man. As far as my writing is concerned, he is fine with whatever I would like to share with him and if I choose to share nothing he is fine

I was once worried about what would happen if my book were published and it became a success and how I would not want to be in the spotlight. Johnny said, "Life is simple. Just like a garage door opener. Button makes it go up, then down. That's it"

Johnny and I got married on September 2nd 2012 which is also his birthday. We had a private ceremony in our home and a small reception afterwards with 87 of our nearest and dearest family and friends in attendance. My father gave a speech saying that out of all the places I'd been to in the world I had to find Johnny in literally the backyard of my home. Everyone had a big laugh over that. That is true love.

I married a simple man who brings joy to me and everyone around him. His life consists of waking up early, having a cup of coffee, running small errands. He is a man who never has a plan; he does what he feels like in the moment. If he feels like cooking a special dinner, he'll go to the grocery store. Sometimes he goes to the grocery store every day. He is not concerned about planning in advance, after all the grocery store isn't going anywhere.

To those who know Johnny he is a prankster and a jokester with a heart of gold. We virtually have no hobbies in common except for baseball but we laugh and smile each day and our love grows stronger with each passing day.

If you are a single man or woman reading this know and believe that somewhere out there is a Johnny or an Apara waiting for you. Just remember that human love, just like animal love, should produce calm, provide warmth and relaxation in an environment of trust while wanting nothing in return.

A friend once told me, "Your love for each other tells a thousand stories." This is the short story I wrote about meeting Johnny in Jimmy's Deli.

"The Power of Coffee"

To the outside world, Jimmy's Deli is a building made of bricks and mortar. The exterior is not attractive, inviting or even special. It's just an ordinary building nestled among other ordinary buildings on Main Street USA.

I had passed Jimmy's Deli on many occasions but never thought of going inside until I was told, "If you want good coffee, go to Jimmy's Deli."

The first time I entered Jimmy's Deli I was greeted by Jimmy and his wife with a smile, a warm welcome and a coffee. Upon taking my first sip, I realized that Jimmy's coffee wasn't just good coffee; it was the *best coffee* I had ever tasted which made me keep coming back for more. With the same intensity and curiosity as one would ponder the meaning of life, many times I thought why is Jimmy's coffee so good? Does it have to do with the brand of coffee? The coffee pot? The way it's brewed? The sugar? I never could figure out the reason. I just kept coming back for more coffee.

After a few visits I became a "regular." There are no set criteria or requirements for becoming a "regular" at Jimmy's Deli. Becoming a "regular" just seems to automatically happen and you are accepted as a "regular" just by consistently showing up. Whether you are a regular or not, you are treated as an equal. In a world where the judgment of others is abundant, at Jimmy's Deli a utopian society exists where age, sex, race, religion, culture, education or political affiliation simply does not matter. Everyone is respected. Everyone is welcome. Everyone is noticed. Everyone wants Jimmy's coffee.

The reasons why people come to Jimmy's Deli are not important but the door they walk through means everything.

The arrival of someone is announced either by the chime of the bell on the front door or the slam of the back door. In the entertainment industry the "stars" or "people who want to be noticed" enter and exit through the back door while the audience enters through the front door. Though Jimmy's Deli is not a celebrity venue it does have its share of entertainers and the entertainers, all true to form, enter through the back door.

Just as people don't want to miss an episode of their favorite television show, you don't want to miss an episode of "Jimmy's Deli." Everything is live and no one knows beforehand what the show will be about. There are no rehearsals or scripts involved and there are no previews for the upcoming episode. To find out what happens next you have to come back the next day. For 30 minutes and $1.50 (cost of a medium cup of coffee) you can sit back, relax and enjoy the show as it unfolds.

"The Silent and Speaker Show" airs Monday through Friday with an occasional episode on Saturday. Back door opens with gusto. Speaker enters first. Silent follows. They take their designated seats at the counter and the show begins. Speaker, the main character, does not drink coffee so he orders tea with a lot of sugar. Silent, Speaker's sidekick, orders coffee. Once beverages are in hand the show begins. Speaker speaks – nonstop – about anything and everything. Speaker is animated, lively and loud. Silent speaks only when he has something to say or when he can seize an opportunity to say something when Speaker has his mouth full of food. No matter what the topic, the "Silent and Speaker Show" makes everyone laugh and smile. At the conclusion of each episode Silent and Speaker exit just as they entered – though the back door.

"Tell It Like It Is with Mr. Baseball" airs Saturday mornings. Back door opens and in walks Mr. Baseball. Mr. Baseball's first order of business is to get his cup of coffee. As he is the star of his show, Mr. Baseball drinks his coffee out of a brown ceramic mug while the audience members drink their coffees out of plain Styrofoam cups. At the beginning of each episode Mr. Baseball reads the sports section of the newspaper informing his audience of relevant sport news and games of the day. The next portion of his show is open discussion with the audience where no topic is off-limits. When Mr. Baseball has something to say he just "tells it like it is" which is usually his uncensored opinion on whatever topic is being discussed. "Tell It Like

It Is with Mr. Baseball" is definitely not a children's show and, luckily, children are not normally around when his show is airing.

In between episodes there are also brief commercial breaks which are equally as entertaining.

"Mr. Fix-It" walks in the back door several times a day informing the audience members about restaurant equipment, motor issues or car problems. The "Mr. Fix-It" commercials are usually brief and, once his advertisement is finished, he exits through the back door coffee in hand.

"Mr. Tornado" is a public service announcement reminding everyone to always be alert and prepared for the unexpected because you cannot predict when a tornado will strike. No one knows when the "Mr. Tornado" ad will air but when he enters through the back door, swift winds are felt as he shuts the door quickly and rushes in. "Mr. Tornado" is constantly on the move. Once his food order is ready he is out the back door and everyone feels the wake of the door opening and closing.

Though all the shows and commercials are not alike no show can go one without a cup of Jimmy's coffee.

I was told on more than one occasion to try coffee at another establishment because that coffee was good. So I tried it. To me, it tasted like coffee, neither good nor bad. The owner of the establishment insisted that the coffee in my cup was old and had me replenish my cup from a freshly made pot. I took a sip and, once again, it was just coffee. The owner said I should come in the morning when the pots are freshly brewed and sold out by the hundreds. I will not because I know it will be nothing more than coffee.

Good coffee can be found anywhere but the best coffee can only be found at Jimmy's Deli.

Johnny and I on our wedding day in 2012

Chapter 18

The Blue Pen

"Fear is like a hologram. It seems real, filled with substance. And then, when you go beyond it, you realize there is nothing there. It's all an illusion."

- Ambulance Girl, 2005

Ambulance Girl is a movie based on a book of the same name by Jane Stern. Jane is a food writer who conquered her depression and became a paramedic. Jane is my inspiration as well as a man named John.

Having worked in the emergency room at the medical center for a number of years I decided to take another leap of blind faith and join my small town's rescue squad. I didn't find them; they found me.

One night I was sitting at my desk by the ambulance bay when a rescue squad appeared and handed me a slip of paper with their patient's information to input. I did not immediately look up but when I did I saw the friendly faces of my town's own rescue squad. Looking at them, I felt like I wanted to be a part of them and one of their friendly faces helping to transport people to the hospital.

There was a man named John who worked at the hospital as an EMT (Emergency Medical Technician) who was also a member of the squad. Shortly after my encounter with the squad I ran into John and told him I was thinking about joining the squad but had some questions. John handed me his business card and on it was a social media page link. When I looked at the site I learned it was for a charity dedicated to John's son Alex who had died of cancer four years earlier. That night I read the entire social media page including several letters John had written to Alex. One sentence in one letter hit me like a ton of bricks:

"You made me promise to never go back to a job that I hated, so I didn't. I'm an EMT now and all I do is help people."

I read and reread that sentence the entire night. That had been me. I had been in jobs I loved and jobs I hated but never really found a true home that I wanted to be in, a place where I could help others.

During times of unemployment my father tried to guide me and always wished that I had a mentor like he had throughout his career. From that moment on I knew I had found the mentor in John whom my father had always wanted for me. I wanted to be an EMT just like John. Alex wanted to be on the rescue squad prior to his passing. I also wanted to be like Alex.

A few weeks later I applied to be a member of the rescue squad and was accepted. I got trained on where all medical supplies were on the ambulance or "rig" as it was commonly called. My role was to be assistant and when I was on duty I was to just do whatever was asked of me whether it be to write down the patient's information or simply carry the medical supply bag.

Whenever my pager went off I got dressed as quickly as a fireman and raced to the squad building to get on the ambulance with the rest of my duty night crew. On the way to the squad building I always prayed that I would do everything ok.

I almost quit the squad once. Right when I turned forty Johnny and I had just returned from a trip to India with my parents. There was a lot of stress prior to the trip and somehow the night of my fortieth birthday I became afraid that I would just not be in the right mindset three days later when I would be on call. I'm no quitter but at that time I didn't see any other option.

The president of the squad reached out to me via text message and talked me through my fears. He gave me the option of taking a short leave of absence so that I could regroup myself and come back refreshed. Quitting the squad would have been the biggest mistake of my life but thanks to my "squad angel", as I call the president, he cared enough to talk me through. For this I am grateful.

Another fear I had regarding the squad was what if I wasn't able to find something on the ambulance when it was needed. Yes, that is correct. Blood and bodily injuries do not scare me but not being able to find an item which may be needed by our EMT did.

Ed is a police officer in my town who I occasionally run into on squad calls. Ed is also a friend who, by mere virtue of knowing me, believes that one day I will become a good EMT. Our police are always present on calls. The first call I was ever on with Ed he asked me for a non rebreather (breathing mask) from the ambulance. I had no idea what he was talking about. I found the non rebreather after a few minutes but felt like a complete idiot in the process, especially in front of my friend.

One Friday night in August was the night I can say that all of my fears went away.

My squad pager sounded and I received a text message on my phone from an automated system that it was a call for an overdose. Without thinking I got dressed as quickly as possible not even putting my socks on and raced to the call. I just knew I had to be on this call.

The patient, a man, was alert but starting to fade in and out and during the ambulance ride to the hospital I kept talking to him, asking him to tell me about himself. I knew I had to keep him awake and talking. He told me that he was an artist and when I asked him what he drew he told me angels and demons. I could relate to angels and demons very well.

While talking with this man I looked straight into his eyes and in them I saw myself; I stared into the face of humanity. He could have been me, or anyone battling a chemical imbalance.

The funny thing about this particular call was it could have been my worst fear on the ambulance come to reality yet everything went perfectly. Anything that was asked for by the crew I was able to find with ease right down to a single blue pen which someone was looking for but only I saw.

I have to ensure that I can go to EMT school and balance out stress with regard to my mania but it's heartwarming to have both Ed and John believe in me so much that, even if I never become an EMT, is enough.

As for fear, it's really is just an illusion. After all, I did find the blue pen when no one else could just as I found the needle in the haystack. It was just there all along.

Chapter 19

Grief Is the Price We Pay for Love

"You're in the arms of the angel. May you find some comfort here."

-"Angel" by Sarah McLachlan

Death is a part of life. There is no denying this fact. The pain of death is compounded by the deep love we feel towards other human beings and even our animal companion friends.

Several years ago there was a mother cat in New York who saved her kittens from a burning structure. The mother cat was later adopted by a woman named Karen. I once wrote something about loss to Karen on social media, and she responded to me:

"Grief is the price we pay for love."

How true. How profound. The deeper we love, the deeper we grieve. However, if given the choice, would we ever sacrifice love to spare grief? I don't think anyone would.

When I was diagnosed with Manic Bipolar, I just accepted. I didn't grieve for a life I thought I had but lost. I moved on with the life that was now to be. There was once a time where I had no chemical imbalance, and my life was a certain way. Then, when I was diagnosed with mania, my old life died and a new one was reborn. I wouldn't say I grieved for the way I used to be though. I was blessed for what I was and the fact that, through medication, my brain could be healthy.

My Manic Bipolar diagnosis was a death of sorts; a death of an old way of living. Lithium, my protective shield, gave me a new lease on life.

I shared with you my stories of my cat Zhangy and my grandfather. Though Zhangy was a cat and my grandfather was a human being, both were living creatures and I grieved for both equally, until I was able to memorialize their lives permanently in my stories through my deep love for them.

Zhangy and my grandfather are losses, no more, no less, and the grief and love are equal.

I'd like to share an email between my father and a good friend whose cat had died in a tragic accident:

My father: "We are very sorry to learn about one of your cats. Pets are family members and the loss hurts. While there is no real explanation of why life comes and goes, Eastern philosophy would say that the time had come or it was meant to be this way. Therefore, don't feel guilty."

My friend: "Thanks for your sympathy. I never could imagine that it would hurt that much, especially when thinking about the way she died and I'll never forget what I saw when I opened my bedroom door yesterday. I very much hope she'll forgive me. I feel I had to learn something really important through this and I'm sure I did."

Is there a lesson to be learned from the death of another, animal or human? I believe the lesson is to show us how vast our hearts are and their capability to love. Pain and grief are nothing more than love turned upside down.

I did not die on February 9th 2010, and every day I celebrate the new lease on life I was given. Even in death, I believe there should be joy, laughter and celebration of a life well lived. When Whitney Houston passed away I watched her funeral on television. I admired the big sendoff and celebration of life. When someone passes I believe we should celebrate. Grieve, yes, but do not mourn for the life lost, celebrate the life lived with a "Life Sendoff."

Johnny and I have occasionally talked about what we would like our "Life Sendoff" to be like. For his I imagine a scene from the movie "P.S. I Love You," where the Pogues' "Fairytale of New York" is playing and everyone drinks shots in cheer and celebration. Johnny says he wants a closed casket so no one will touch him. Haha…fine by me. I'll put the Johnny Walker bottles and shot glasses atop his casket. I believe I'll sing along to "Fairytale of New York" too since Johnny loves making fun of my singing. He'll surely be looking at his "Life Sendoff" from above and laughing along with all of us for sure.

Inside his casket, in his arms, he will be holding the ashes of my beloved little Zhangy, my little Soul Cat. Johnny knew Zhangy for six months and knew how special he was to me. It would only be befitting that Johnny take my Zhangy, a piece of my heart, in the ground with him.

As for me, I'd like my body to go to a medical school so that students may learn from me, even by dissecting my mind. I never became a doctor but I would want this to be my thanks to the medical profession for developing the medications to keep me, and this book, going. Maybe my mind will help to find a cure for mania and other chemical imbalances. That would be the greatest gift I could ever give.

Is it morbid to talk about your own funeral while you're still alive? Absolutely not! If you don't tell people what you want, how will they ever know?

I must speak in this chapter of suicide as I know people whose loved ones have chosen to take their own life. I can only speak for the "alien" in my head, but if someone is suffering from depression or another chemical imbalance and if they are not on medication or the medication is not working, then their actions are not their own. For anyone who has suffered the loss of a suicide and are blaming yourself for not doing enough, just your love and support of that person was enough. What was going on in their head was simply out of their control and yours. For your loss I am sorry and I grieve with you.

When I started this book, Robin Williams had just committed suicide and I, like the rest of the nation, was shocked. The media spoke about all his famous movies, except for a little-known film of his which is my absolute favorite, called "What Dreams May Come." This film is basically about heaven, hell and the afterlife and, after watching this film, it's what I believe heaven to be like.

I apologize now for giving away the plot if you have not yet seen this amazing film, but the wife and soulmate of Robin's character commits suicide. When he finds out, his pain is unbearable to watch on the screen – it surpassed "good acting." It is ironic Robin Williams chose to end his own life but, even without knowing all the facts about what was going through his mind, I know it was the "alien" and not him nor his free will.

The day after his death, I heard a news commentator say that performers on medication say it dulls the mania and dulls the talent. In a way I could relate, as four and a half years went by before I attempted to write anything again. If anything, this book serves as a testament to the fact that it is possible to revive talent even with medication.

I wish Robin Williams could have taken a year off to get back on medication, rest and rediscover himself and his talents on the medication. Even before he would have been missed, I know he would have been back in the spotlight bigger and better than ever. To those who loved Robin Williams, his death was not in vain, and this book is testament to that fact.

John, my EMT friend who lost his son Alex to cancer, taught me that love never ends. Alex is always with John as he works as an EMT and on the cancer charity he began in Alex's name, Alex4Ever.

Just because someone, whether it be human or animal, is no longer with us, our love for them really does never end.

May you find some comfort in this passage. I do believe in angels and that all of our departed loved ones are now in the arms of the angels and watching over us.

Chapter 20

Let's Keep the Stigma Alive, Shall We?

"What some folks call impossible, is just stuff they haven't seen before"

- What Dreams May Come, 1998

I can't help reverting back to Robin Williams and his tragic passing. Whenever there is a news story of a celebrity death, such as this one, the media talks about bringing attention and awareness to depression, suicide, resources for help and removal of stigma etc.

When the news broke with how Williams ended his life, my mother said she didn't know why the news had to mention that and people didn't need to know that. I said that because he was a celebrity his life, sadly, was an open book. My mother repeated that people didn't need to know. It's, unfortunately, the price you pay for fame and fortune.

To quote Johnny when I speak about something that doesn't interest him:

"Alls I hear is blah blah blah"

When I listened to the news about removing stigmas all I heard was blah blah blah.

It's all bullshit.

After a few days, something else will take over the news and everyone will conveniently forget what it was they brought attention to that was so important, hence we keep the stigma of mental illness and chemical imbalances alive and kicking.

I am not a medical professional. I am not a psychiatrist, psychologist or mental health professional. Aside from being a mental patient, for lack of a better word (as there is no better word), I have no affiliation to the mental health world.

As a human being with Manic Bipolar, here's what I would suggest.

Don't call it mental Illness. Abolish and banish that word. Make it obsolete. Make it disappear. How about calling it Chemical Imbalance Syndrome or Mind Imbalance Disorder. The word "mental" is misused, mislabeled, abused and has nothing but negativity associated with it. It needs to go.

My father is an expert trainer in his field and people pay him to conduct training sessions. He and his knowledge are valued commodities. Our minds are valued commodities too, yet if you tell someone you are seeing a therapist you may ultimately receive the "crazy" label. There's no difference between what my father does and a therapist does: Provides expertise for a fee. Yet it's ok for someone to say I'm going to XYZ training session but not ok to say I'm going to my therapist.

I was blessed to have had an excellent therapist in the time I needed her in order to figure out who this "new me" was post-diagnosis.

At the hospital where I worked, I once had a conversation with a mental health worker. I had just recently gone parasailing and was talking about my experience. The best way I could describe parasailing to her was that it was just like "touching heaven." In response she made a light joke alluding to the fact that maybe I belonged with the mental patients. I kept quiet. Its one thing to tell someone "I'm not Asian; I'm half Indian and half Eastern European." It's quite another to tell someone "I have Manic Bipolar and your joke bothered me." In one scenario, you just make a correction and clarification. In the other, you get labeled "crazy."

This same woman loves my hairstyle. She seems to be obsessed with my hair, as a matter of fact. Each time she sees me, day after day without fail, she tell me "I love your hair." Next day: "I love your hair." Next day: "I love your hair."

Now, you tell me, who is the crazy one here?

I don't want to slight this woman in any
way, because she is a lovely and caring person, but I had to
use this as an example to bring my point home.

I've encountered many psychiatric patients in my
career and I've heard many of them, when first brought
into the emergency room, speaking about God, angels and
demons. I understand perfectly what they mean though
everyone else thinks they are "crazy." To have a brain free
of chemical imbalance is an angel. To have mania,
depression or any other chemical imbalance which, if left
untreated, wreaks havoc in your life is truly a
demon. There's just no better way of putting it.

I have been involuntarily committed to mental
institutions twice in my life; the first when I had a severe
manic episode when my mania was diagnosed. The second
was when I let my book writing get to my head, literally.
I'm not ashamed to talk about these experiences. The first
time I was put on Lithium. The second I was put on a low
dose mood stabilizer for a short period of time until my
insomnia went away. When our bodies need treatment we
go to the hospital for diabetes and cancer, body ailments.
Mental hospitals treat brain ailments and I have no shame
in saying I've been to one twice because those facilities
curbed the "alien" in my head and made my protective

shield stronger.

Have you ever used the word anon in your daily vocabulary? Anon is actually an obsolete word meaning at once or immediately. I stumbled upon this word by accident while researching obsolete words but it's quite appropriate.

At one time I was even going to author this book as by Anon Person, aka anonymous person. That's right; share my wonderful life and stories all with no identifying details right down to calling myself essentially a nobody, all because I was afraid to admit that I have a mental illness. But I'm not afraid of anything anymore, and I refuse to hide myself and my wonderful stories to the world under a badge of shame that society created and refuses to change.

If my book were to have a theme song, it would be "Love and Understanding" by Cher because that is my ultimate message:

We got enough stars to light the sky at night
Enough sun to make to make the whole world bright
We got more than enough
But there's one thing there's just not enough of

    Not enough love and understanding
We could use some love to ease these troubled
times
Not enough love and understanding
Why, oh why?

    Love and understanding. That's all it takes. Love
and understanding.

Chapter 21

Book of Possibilities, Not Buckets

I've never been a fan of the term bucket list, a list of things to do before you die. Why would anyone want to plan for their death when each and every day brings forth new and wondrous possibilities?

Instead of bucket list I have an activities wish list; activities and places I'd like Johnny and me to do at some point. But, if we don't get around to them, that's okay too. There's no "death deadline" so it doesn't matter. I also have a book of possibilities.

In the 2006 movie "Last Holiday" starring Queen Latifah, her character finds out that she has a fatal disease so she decides to "blow" all of her spending and go somewhere she's always wanted to go, her dream place. She also has a scrapbook in which she has a collage of all the things she wants to do in her life, which she calls the book of possibilities.

Did all of her wishes come true, including what was in the book of possibilities? Yes they did, and more!

I didn't actually have a book of possibilities until I

started writing this book. I do not have a scrapbook as Queen Latifah's character did in the movie, but here's what I have:

I would like "Angel Child" to be published. I would like my book to make a difference in someone's life, even if only one person reads it and it touches them. This would be my one dream come true.

I want everyone who has touched my life in some way, shape or form to receive a copy of "Angel Child," especially those living I mentioned throughout the book. I do not know where my first love, Robert Vargas, is living but most of all I want a copy to reach his hands.

Would I want "Angel Child" to be a best seller? Could a book about an ordinary person with an extraordinary gift of writing who overcame her struggles and shared her story of mind over mania wins make it to the top? That would be wonderful because then my message of love and understanding would reach millions of lives.

Do I want to make a fortune having my book be No. 1 on the New York Times best seller list? Money would be nice. There are a few charities I wouldn't mind writing out a big fat donation check to.

I also wouldn't mind a nice exotic vacation with Johnny to celebrate. I would leave the destination choice to

Johnny, but if I were to choose I would love to visit Tokyo and, especially, Kyoto to see the last remaining Geisha women as Geisha culture has always fascinated me.

I would love to be a guest on the Ellen Degeneres show to promote my book. I want to make my entrance dancing to Cher's "Love and Understanding" alongside Ellen as she loves to dance as much as I do. That would be so much fun and Johnny would have fun laughing at the way I dance on national television.

Who knows what could happen? There's nothing wrong with dreaming big and having a book of possibilities. I've had so many dreams come to fruition thus far. A few more can't hurt.

Most important of all, well above fame and fortune, is that I would like to have a life of mediocrity. Yes, you heard correctly, a life of mediocrity. My mind is my most precious commodity, and preserving it is of utmost importance. I wouldn't want anything to be too much where it would "go to my head" and once again end up in a mental treatment facility for insomnia or exhaustion. My protective shield against the "alien" will always come first.

Chapter 22

My Happy Medium

I work on one chapter per day. I constantly have music playing, usually a song which reminds me of the particular passage I'm working on. I find there is a song to match every mood and situation. Sometimes I sing while writing. Sometimes I get up and dance a little and Johnny teases me for doing so in his loving way. Mostly, though, what keeps me focused is pretending I'm writing these stories to you, my best friend. I make my writing fun because it is fun, as long as it doesn't become a hypomanic episode.

Under my shield of protection from the alien now lies a lockbox. Whenever I have an idea for a story or a book chapter I immediately file my ideas into the lockbox. Whenever I am ready to write, I open the lockbox and pull them out. My story ideas can remain in my lockbox for months, but they are there and not going anywhere.

There is no race. The golden egg will always be there. I still have to remind myself of this on occasion.

I don't know if this will be my last book but, if it is, the ride I've been on to write it and all the bumps in the road have been worth it.

Despite the odds I managed to write creatively in moderation to incorporate the stories of my life in to what I call my masterpiece. When you have a masterpiece completed, it becomes quite hard to try and top it. It took me a little over a month to compile and complete this book.

The one thing I am proud of is that I was able to write about myself and my mania without fear; fear, that is, of being judged by others. There are millions of people out there suffering from mental illnesses and chemical imbalances, and if my stories can touch and inspire even one person, then it would have all been worth it.

I don't generally make plans on the day I am on call so that I am well-rested and refreshed. With my free time I write throughout the day. I generally have the television on mute so I can occasionally peer up at something without the sound distracting me. When writing I always have music playing, usually a song reminiscent of the piece that I'm working on. I sometimes sing and dance as well. My life is a continuous check and balance of my protective shield, one I am determined to never have crack again.

Writing became overwhelming at times and I occasionally lost focus. If I found myself having more than two chapter documents open at once on my computer, I would close them both and walk away. That's what I needed to do. Other times I would stumble upon tidbits of information from the "archives of my life," which I was tempted to start using but had to file away for another time. Discipline. Discipline. Discipline. In the end I came to the conclusion that if something were meant to be in this book it would find its way.

All I can say is that most people get a hell of a lot more than they bargained for when I enter their lives. They say that honesty is the best policy, and I have nothing to lose by being honest and taking a blind leap of faith in sharing myself with the world.

Chapter 23

Ordinary Person

I am an ordinary person walking among you. I could be your sister, your best friend, a colleague or just someone you pass by on the street. What you don't know is that I am a writer with a slight touch of mania, and that has made all the difference. I'm not afraid to admit that I have mania and I'm not afraid to share my incredible journey as to how I wrote this book with you.

All my life I've been a writer. It's a gift I somehow acquired which I try to put to good use. I used to write short stories which I would share with family and friends and those interested. Many encouraged me to try and have my stories published but I never actively pursued it.

Over the years a shared a select few of my stories with certain persons in my life whom I felt would appreciate them. All the rest I kept all to myself; my hoard, my secret stash.

Never in my wildest dreams could I have imagined publishing a book. Had someone predicted this I surely would have laughed in their face. Now it's a reality and I've made the impossible possible, as I have made so many other things in my life come to fruition.

I once was afraid to write again; afraid that the mania would come out instead. It did, but as with all other challenges in my life, I overcame it.

One day I shared a short story with a friend and told my friend "Once upon a time, I used to write short stories. Some people even thought they were good. I don't have the ability to write short stories any more but I've got plenty to look back on."

In response my friend told me:

"Hey, you're writing. It's not dead."

My friend used an interesting word because I never said that my writing was dead. But, I used mania as a crutch, as an excuse, to not write all these years. My friend's comment to me changed the world as I knew it at that very moment.

In order to write this book I had to face my greatest fear well beyond people knowing that I had mania; I had to face mania itself head on, embrace it, and make it a part of my heart. Then and only then was I able to write my masterpiece which is this book.

Because of my friend's encouragement I started to write stories again and it was good. My mind not having an "off" switch when it was time to go to bed was not good but it was a lesson learned and I am recovered from it.

Writing is my soulmate. It is my deepest love from the core of my being. It is a gift. It is my greatest love and my deepest heartache. One could even say writing is both my angel and my demon.

Chapter 24

Angel Child

I am Angel Child. I walk among you day after day. Sometimes you notice me. Other times you don't.

I am human. I don't claim to be anything more. I've been through life's ups and downs, just like you.

My life is a gift and so is yours. This book, "Angel Child," is my gift to you.

Life is like a monumental birthday party where a table is set aside for the placement of gifts. Gifts are placed on the table, all for the recipient. When there is no more room, a second layer of gifts is piled on top of the first. No one takes any away. All the stories in "Angel Child," therefore, are your gifts to keep.

For me, Angel Child is my departed loved ones such as my grandfather, my cat Zhangy, Mrs. Farmer and Mrs. Weber. Angel Child is my parents, friends and Johnny most of all. It's John and Ed. Angel Child is anyone who has touched me profoundly in my life, believed in me, loved me. Angel Child is anyone I've helped in my life and anyone who has put a smile on my face and anyone for whom I've put a smile on their face.

Angel Child is a day at the beach, my happy place. It's your happy place and the people who have in some way touched all of your lives, all rolled in to one.

Most of all, Angel Child is the face of humanity. Angel Child is in each and every person you encounter even as a passerby on the street. All the faces of humanity. One day Angel Child was a man randomly waving at me while driving by and blasting Cher's Love and Understanding on my radio.

Angel Child is from my heart and I give it to you from my heart. I wrote it for myself and to inspire others through my stories, especially those living under the stigma of chemical imbalances. I wrote it for anyone who may lose hope, to know that there is something to live for, something to look forward to, something to remember and believe in whenever the challenges and bumps of life get you down.

Keep Angel Child with you always, especially if your hope is gone. Angel Child will inspire you. Keep Angel Child close, on your shoulder, and in your heart always. Make Angel Child a part of you.

Be an Angel Child to someone. You never know when putting a smile on someone's face will change their world.

Be an Angel Child to yourself. Smile and change the world. I did it. So can you.

Love,

Apara

Acknowledgements

To Christi Kelly and Kate Price, Editors extraordinaire. Without you Angel Child would never have been published and I am grateful to you and all of your efforts more than you know, times infinity.

To CreateSpace.com for easily making my dream of publishing a book a reality.

To Inez, Eileen, Annemarie, Rosanne, Keith and John my beta readers. Your encouragement of my words meant the world to me, more than you know, times infinity.

To Johnny, my husband, my soulmate. You fell in love with me through my writing which is why you never sent that baseball card back. You are my coach and my champion, just as "the Chief" was to you. He's smiling down at you from heaven now because his Angel Child got into the Cooperstown Hall of Fame. You made the Chief proud. You make me proud to be your wife. I love you more than you know, times infinity.

To my parents Millie and Artie Mahal. Your daughter wrote a book, something you, Papa, always believed I could do. I did it and Johnny helped like he always helps. I know you are proud of us.

To everyone in my life who loves me, encourages me and inspires me every day. I did not tell many people I was writing a book yet without all of you contributing to who I am today this book would not have been possible. You are all my Angel Child.

Last but never least, to my best friend. You told me I should write books. In a chance encounter you told me my writing was not dead. You were right but only through your belief in me was my writing reborn. Despite all my challenges it was because of you that my writing became alive again. You are my Angel Child and Angel Child would not have been possible without you. I love you and the one I describe as "to know her is to love her" more than you know, times infinity, and beyond.

Website: www.angelchildapara.com

19282862R00094

Made in the USA
Middletown, DE
11 April 2015